Spiritual Reflections On Everyday Life

by Father Bill Stelling

Eagle Wing Books, Inc.
Memphis, Tennessee

Spiritual Reflections On Everyday Life

Copyright © 1998 by William Stelling

All rights reserved. Printed in the United States.

No part of this publication may be reproduced or transmitted in any form of by any means, electronic or mechanical, including photocopy, recording, or any other information storage and retrieval system now known or to be invented, without permission, in writing, from the publisher or author, except by a reviewer who wishes to quote brief passages in connection with a review written for inclusion in a newspaper, magazine, book, or broadcast.

Published in the United States by Eagle Wing Books, Inc.

Address inquiries to:
    Eagle Wing Books, Inc.
    Post Office Box 9972
    Memphis, TN 38190

ISBN: 0-940829-23-1

Retail Price: $10.00

First USA printing October 1998.

Dedication

This book is dedicated to all who have fed my spiritual hunger. To all who have offered me room and board along my spiritual journey. *Thank You* — *Father Bill*

Table of Contents

Preface 1
Foreword: Three Days in Paris 3
1 — Spirituality 6
2 — Termites in My Spiritual Life 9
3 — How'd I Get to be Me? 12
4 — Poor George 15
5 — Say It Ain't So, Say It Ain't So!! 18
6 — If a Tree Fell in the Forest 21
7 — Becky's Mom & Serenity 24
8 — Why the Wealthy Aren't Happy 27
9 — If God's So Good, Why's Everything So Bad? 30
10 — It Pays to Advertise 33
11 — Where Do Obligations Come From? 36
12 — Magy's Christmas Story 39
13 — Meekness and Humility!! - As a Solution? 42
14 — Winning Isn't Everything, it's... 45
15 — It Takes Two Hands to Handle a Whopper 48
16 — The Parking Place 51
17 — The Little Man Upon the Stair 54
18 — Now It's Up to You, God 57
19 — What's Holding You Back? 60
20 — Why Does God Love Me? 63
21 — Good Fences Make Good Neighbors? 66
22 — Don't Shoot the Wounded! 69
23 — What Can I Do? 72
24 — When Love Isn't Love 75
25 — At School in the Gutter 78
26 — How Strange - It's Ordinary 81

27 — I'm a Crack(ed) Pot	84
28 — "Trust Me," He Said.	87
29 — Nobody Likes a 'Do Gooder'	90
30 — But in the Real World	93
31 — I Touch the Future - I Teach	96
32 — The Lesson of the Forgotten Wallet	99
33 — Freedom is in the Little Things	102
34 — Climbing Down the Mountains	105
35 — Is the Holy Spirit a Parakeet?	108
36 — What in the World is Grace?	111
37 — "Why" is More Important Than "When"	114
38 — Butterflies in My Heart	117
39 — Emily Was a Good Ole Gal	120
40 — As Long as We Remember ... Huh??	123
41 — College Kids Kill Their Baby!!	126
42 — Bought and Paid For	129
43 — Surrendering isn't Quitting!!	132
44 — A Lesson in Letting Go	135
45 — Fighting With the Life Guard	138
46 — What's So Real About Mary?	141
47 — Hold, Please	144
48 — Forgive? How?	147
49 — A Lesson in Living and Dying	150
50 — Dat's My Daddy!!	153
51 — Death with Dignity, or Dignity with Death	156
52 — Don't Bother Me!!	159
Afterword — Why Should God Remember Me?	162
Index	165

PREFACE

This book was going to be a collection of 52 of the columns I had written over the last eight years. The idea was that perhaps the reader could use one as a point of reflection each week of the year. Since my column, *From the Heart and Mind of Father Bill*, appears weekly in the **West Tennessee Catholic** (formerly known as **Common Sense**) there were almost 400 to choose from. I found the task of selecting 52 much more difficult than I expected. My first attempt yielded 95. That was reduced to 63, and finally to 54. So the book will be a collection of 52 plus 2. The two extra columns were chosen by the publisher as a Foreword and Afterword. My column basically has been a sharing of my spiritual journey. This means that I have not written a "How You Should Book," but a "How I Do Book."

The columns relate what went on in my life at specific times and places, and with particular people. I hold these times, places, and people to have been essential to my spiritual journey. For this reason I have resisted advice to delete these particulars in an effort to make this book more generic.

I have reviewed this collection and found that from time to time lessons, or quotations that I value, have been mentioned more than once. This is not because I forgot that I had mentioned it before, but because they are important to me. As much as possible I am presenting the columns pretty much as I wrote them. The order in which they appear is also the order in which I wrote them with a few exceptions. Naturally, in making the selection there are often gaps in time from one column to the next.

This collection of my columns is offered in the same spirit as each column was written. I can not tell you how to make your spiritual journey. I can only share with how I'm making mine. My spiritual journey is not something I'll complete, or perfect by a certain date, or even in this life. That used to worry me. My spiritual journey is not something that I can plan very far ahead. I find that most often, *one day at a time* works for me. Sometimes, even that's looking too far ahead. That used to *really* worry me. Sometimes it still does.

I realize that everything I've written applies primarily to me, not to you. I'm happy to share with you. It has helped my spiritual journey very much just writing these columns and that's a blessing. If you find them helpful, that's a double blessing.

Foreword

THREE DAYS IN PARIS

Most of the priests of the Diocese enjoyed three days at Paris Landing State Park last week. We were called together by our Bishop for a time of study and fellowship. Our schedule was not full, but it was fulfilling.

Msgr. Warren Holleran from San Francisco, a scripture scholar who teaches at St. Patrick Seminary, led us into the mind and heart of St. Paul. He delved generously into the Gospel and Letters of St. John, and touched lightly on the parables in the Gospels of Matthew, Mark, and Luke. His knowledge of his subject was evident, his love of the scriptures was both compelling and infectious.

The morning sessions on Tuesday and Wednesday were from 9:00 am till 11:30 am. The evening sessions on Monday and Tuesday were from 7:30 pm to 8:45 pm. This may seem long, even with breaks, but with Warren's enthusiasm there were few complaints.

We celebrated the liturgy: Morning Prayer; Mass; and Evening Prayer together. This was the linchpin of our fellowship. However, there were also golf, tennis, trails to hike, swimming, bridge, and meals that drew groups, both large, and small together.

One of the highlights of our time together was the Mass and Dinner at Holy Cross parish in Paris. When our Days of Study and Fellowship are at Paris Landing, Father Victor always invites us all over for a meal. The Knights of Columbus were our hosts.

We alternate from year to year between Pickwick and Paris Landing for these annual Days of Study and Fellowship. Each parish pays only for the priests they send. I've no idea what the total cost is. But this much I do know: There is no way to calculate the total benefit to the Diocese as a whole. So, as far as I'm concerned, it's worth it at twice the price. Whatever that may be.

While at Paris Landing I took a look around me at our priests. I was reminded of the words from that song of the 60's, *"...Where have all the flowers gone."* There were so many who for one reason or another could not be with us, and so many, many who had died. I looked around at the priests who were there and two things struck me, in fact alarmed me. There are so few of us, and there are so many of us with gray hair. I thought of our Bishop's prayer for vocations to the priesthood and religious life that we've started using throughout the diocese. It's not only a beautiful and timely prayer, it's an urgent one also.

We, priests, do have four or five occasions throughout the year to come together for a meeting and a meal, but then, all too quickly, it's back to the parish. Doctors, lawyers, bricklayers, and bankers need the fellowship of others with their own skills, or expertise. But priests, particularly diocesan priests, who do not have the company, the companionship, of a religious community have a definite need for each other. Not only for strength and scholarship, but simply for the fellowship provided by golf, tennis, swimming, hiking, bridge, meals together, and so.

All in all, it was a good time, a very good time, and I look forward to our next three days together in Paris.

This column is somewhat shorter than I thought it'd be, so I'll tell you about a letter I received from *"A Subscriber."* The writer, who made no other identification, took umbrage at my use of: "gonna," "feller," and "ya" as in: "A feller told me this the other day, and I'm gonna share it with ya now."

The writer encouraged me to stop trying to be *"one of the boys"* and, *"to use proper English so that you may be influential in helping your readers to use the proper spelling in their future lives."* The writer enclosed a copy of my column, **Something of Value** in which I said, "So the way I see it, my job ... is teaching."

I have no idea who the writer is. I'll admit I did lay claim to the title of *teacher*, but I don't teach grammar. I'm not trying to be one of the boys, I am trying to teach the Good News of the Lord Jesus Christ as I experience it. However, if by using proper grammar and helping my readers use the proper spelling in their future lives I'll also help them to rejoice in the Good News of the Lord Jesus, then I'm all for it. I kinda doubt it though. None-the-less, I'm gonna give what this feller has written me some serious thought, don't ya see.

1 — SPIRITUALITY

Because I'm a priest many people have asked me to advise, or help them with their Spirituality. Considering the difficulty I've had with my own Spiritual Life, I've often been reluctant to do so. I'll share with you what happens in my life.

In dealing with Spirituality it's best for me to begin with a question. What is Spirituality, or the Spiritual Life, or my Spiritual journey? Webster is not a big help. He defines it as 1) spiritual character, quality, or nature. 2) the jurisdiction, rights, tithes, etc. belonging to the church, or to an ecclesiastic. 3) the fact or state of being incorporeal (without a body). He gives no better insight defining Spiritual. 1) of the spirit or the soul. 2) concerned with the intellect. 3) consisting of spirit, not body. 4) showing much refinement of thought and feeling. 5) of the church, or religion.

These complications remind me of Anthony de Mello's story of the little fish. He was one of several fish in a large aquarium. An older and wiser fish observed him swimming rapidly back and forth across the tank. He swam up next to the little fish and asked, "What are you doing?"

"I was told that a fish needs water to live, and I am looking for the water."

The older fish was not surprised, he'd been through this before. "We're in the water, the water's all around us. That's what we're swimming in."

"You're kidding," said the little fish, with astonishment. "It can't be that simple." With that he swam off to continue his search for the water.

Well, dictionaries and theologians may argue with me, but the way I see it, Spirituality is simply being aware that God is all around me. The depth of my Spirituality goes up and down, and it depends on how I let people, places, things, and events interfere with, or enhance my conscious contact with my God.

What, and Who is God? Now there's a question over which a lot of ink and blood have been spilt. How do I understand God? Let me share with you something I understand about God. I'm sure we have the same God, but you and I are different. So though much will be the same in the way we each understand God, there will be some differences. That's not because God is different, it's because we are.

One thing I understand about my God is that He is Truth. If there is a living person who is all Truth that person would be God. Now there's a whole lot more to what I understand about God, than the simple fact that God is Truth. I'll share a lot of this with you as you go through this book. Right now I'll let you know how my God being Truth effects my Spiritual Life.

There might be a difference between Truth and Honesty, but for my purpose they mean the same thing. I'm not talking about what some people call, "cash register" honesty. I'm not excluding it either, cause it is essential to real honesty.

I'm talking about that honesty that lives in the remote part of my soul. That part that takes courage to venture into because it seems so dark and challenges my preconceived — and comfortable — notions.

Honesty is light at it's very being, so how can my soul be dark where honesty dwells? Ah! It only seems to be dark, because I've grown accustomed to living with my eyes closed. If I opened my eyes I would have to change and grow. If I opened my eyes I'd have to admit that Truth lives in people I don't like, and often in the criticism given me with what I take to be malice. Truth can hurt, so does removing a cancer. Truth also heals.

If I want to grow spiritually, a good place to begin is with a program of rigorous, total honesty. A word of caution. When your spouse asks for your honest opinion — charity and prudence is advised. Don't worry about perfection, strive for progress. Besides, what would you do for an encore if you ever got to be perfect?

2 — TERMITES IN MY SPIRITUAL LIFE

Termites! I saw a swarm of them in the Church last spring. The sight made me sick, and fearful. I thought of the pest control ads on TV. They showed the dreadful damage these little creatures could do in secret. I knew the damage in the Church would be costly. Just picture in your mind the damage termites can do to your house. On the outside everything looks good, but underneath it's rotten, and crumbling. When you imagine that you know how I felt.

It turned out everything was okay. We have a contract with a pest control company. They give us regular treatments, inspections, and a guarantee. They don't really give us those things. We buy 'em.

Termites do their work, or damage in secret. Unless I take real precautions I could wake up one morning to find my house is almost beyond repair.

As you may have guessed, there is a Spiritual point to all of this. I SHOULD BE ALERT TO TERMITES IN MY SPIRITUAL LIFE. Here are some questions I must face: Do I have any devilish termites secretly working to destroy the Spiritual House in which I live? How do I discover them? And, What can I do about them?

As to the first question: Do I have any devilish termites secretly working to destroy the Spiritual House in which I live?

Unless I'm new to the planet, or know nothing of what goes on around me, I'll admit the answer is a resounding YES!!

Peter tells me that the work of evil is not all that secret. *"Stay sober and alert. our opponent, the devil, is prowling like a roaring lion looking for someone to devour."* (I Peter 5:8)

A roaring lion is hardly secret. So what's the connection with the secret work of termites? Only this: The evil of moral termites is so obvious that I become accustomed to it, I overlook it until the damage is so great I think it too painful to repair, so I learn to live with it.

Of course, not all of the work of devilish termites is done in the open. Most is done in secret. The *"secret force of lawlessness is already at work,"* Paul tells me. (II Thes. 2:7) But, to my mind, not even the, *"secret force of lawlessness,"* is the worst work of devilish termites, for this secret force is outside of myself.

The worst work, the most damage done by devilish termites to my spiritual home, is accomplished by the secrets I hold within myself. There's an ancient Christian song that says, *"We all have our secret fears to face, Our minds and motives to amend; We seek your truth, we need your grace, Our living Lord, and present Friend."* "Secret fears to face," "Minds and motives to amend." There's a lot said there. Keeping my fears within, guarding my thoughts, and motives from the light of day, is always dangerous, and often deadly.

Hidden motives, secrets, and fears are the moral equivalent of termites, and they will destroy the spiritual home in which I would like to live, unless they are exposed.

I once heard someone say, *"We are only as sick as the secrets we keep."* In my experience I find that to be true. Secret fears, hidden motives — oh how much energy it takes to keep them secret, and hidden. How much control they have over me as long as they must be hidden. Now, I don't recommend that one go on radio, or TV, and announce to the world one's secret fears, and hidden motives.

The secular world has pest control people to get rid of hidden termites. If I'm sincere in my desire to grow spiritually, I'll soon find the moral equivalent to pest control people to help me overcome the power of secret fears, and hidden motives.

My search will be slow and deliberate, for I'm looking for a person, ordained or lay, whose spirituality I admire. I aim to build a relationship firmly grounded in spirituality. To establish a discipline of meeting on a regular basis, and talk, talk, talk. Talk about anything that helps me to get to know another person who wants to grow spiritually. And pray, pray, pray, and know that the Lord will never deny me, or any one who's looking for a spiritual pest exterminator.

The point is clear to me now. I can not deal with the termites in my spiritual house alone. I know me, and the desire to keep my hidden faults and fears hidden is strong. This issue will have to be faced again and again if I am to make any progress.

3 — HOW'D I GET TO BE ME?

One time Moses asked God, "Who are you?" And God replied, "*I am Who I am.*" Then he added, "*...you shall tell the Israelites: I AM sent me to you.*" He continued, "*This is my name forever; this is my title for all generations.*" (Ex. 3:14-15)

Scripture scholars say that in Hebrew this would be YAHWEH. They also say that because of the respect the Israelites had for the name of God they never wrote it, except without the vowel markings. Because of this it was later mistakenly rendered, Jehovah.

In earlier times the name a person had was meant to describe the person, not merely to distinguish one person from another. As far as I know YAHWEH, or I AM, intends to describe a person without beginning or end, a person who does not have existence from someone else, but IS existence. YAHWEH, or I AM, is the reason that everything else exists, and gives meaning to everything that exists.

Now don't give up on me. I have a point to make, and it's not up in the clouds somewhere.

One time the Scribes and Pharisees asked John, "Who are you?" A series of, "I am nots," constituted most of his answer. Jesus asked his disciples, "Who do people say that I am?"

Recently I asked myself that question. "Who am I?" God's answer to Moses was simplicity itself.

When I tried to answer that question I found myself getting very complicated. I kept adding to a list of characteristics that distinguish me from others. Finally I applied the KISS principle: KEEP IT SIMPLE SWEETHEART.

As Jessie says, "I am somebody." But WHO AM I? Well, I am not, "I AM."

I began to list some characteristics about me that I thought were absolutely necessary for me to be me.

First, since I'm not God I must exist in RELATIONSHIP to someone else. I can go through genealogies till I'm blue in the face, but it all leads back to a cause without a cause — to God. So, as I understand it, there is no way that I can be me unless I relate to God.

Second, I'm human. My NATURE, my ESSENCE is human. Although there are billions of humans, I don't think I could be me unless I was human. And I don't care what the reincarnationalists say.

There are billions of human beings and they all relate to God. I'm convinced that I can not be me without being human and relating to God, so how am I distinguished from all other humans who relate to God? That brings up the third thing.

I'm a PERSON. That is, I get credit or blame for the things I do, or don't do. I have personality, my own unique way of expressing my nature, and relationship to God.

I may be wrong about those three things being THE three things necessary for me to be ME, but that's what I believe. "So what," you may ask, "What's the point?"

Well, the point is that if those are the three things necessary for me to be ME, then I don't have to define myself by my age, sex, race, job, nationality, etc., etc. I don't have to defend myself because I'm not like somebody else. I don't have to resent, or feel threatened by others because they're not like me.

I saw part of a movie recently in which a man died and returned to life as a woman, but as the same person. Then I asked myself, "Could I still be ME if I was a different sex, race, or nationality?" The answer I got was that while these are important characteristics, I could still be me if they were different.

The more I thought about it, the more I realized how really important it is that I know that I am a human being, with a personality, relating to God. If these things come first in my life, then all other characteristics receive the secondary importance they deserve, and I am able to see prejudice of any kind for the phony issue that it is.

4 — POOR GEORGE

Lately I've been remembering a meditation I wrote several years ago. It's called, "POOR GEORGE." It's about the responsibility to speak up, even when it's difficult. It's also about the disastrous results of denial. The meditation begins with words from St. James.

"My brothers, the case may arise among you of someone straying from the truth, and of another bringing him back. Remember this: the person who brings a sinner back from his way will save his soul from death, and cancel a multitude of sins." (James 5:19-20)

POOR GEORGE

Poor George is dead, died last night. Seems odd he should die, wasn't really sick, all he had was a cold, a cold in the head. Least that's what he said.

I 'member when he got it, way back last summer. Just a few sniffles, and a sneeze or two.

George wasn't worried. He was healthy as a horse. Never been sick a day in his life. Oh, he'd had a cold or two, and a smoker's cough, but that wasn't sick, not really.

When summer turned to fall, and the cold stayed with him, some began to worry, and offered their best — hot chicken soup, or, "You better get some rest."

Most everyone said, "Oh it's just a cold George, a cold in the head, everybody gets them, they're common as sin."

But people who had kids told 'em not to get too close. You know how easy kids catch things. As for themselves, they weren't worried, and they told old George, "Don't you worry George, you're not sick, you just got a cold, a cold in the head. What you got, everybody gets, you're as well as any one of us."

Winter came on, and the cold was still there. Some suggested a doctor, but George said, "NO!" He wasn't sick, he just had a cold, a cold in the head. Besides he didn't trust doctors. They'd say he was sick, give him a shot, and put him to bed, and send him a bill, you can count on that.

The doctors, they couldn't agree that he wasn't really sick. But George kept saying that he just had a cold, a cold in the head. All his friends agreed, "George, you're not sick, you just got a cold, a cold in the head. Everybody gets 'em, they're common as sin."

Well, poor George is dead. Died last night. Doc says it's a shame, he'd be alive today, if he'd only known that he was really sick. But we told him, "No, you're not really sick, you just got a cold, a cold in the head. You're just like us, and we're not sick, not sick at all, ARE WE???

NOW WHAT DOES IT MEAN?

Poor George could be any one, and everyone. The cold he has could be sin, or an addiction. His difficulty is in admitting that he is sick, or he has sinned, or is trapped in addiction. Unless George is able to admit that, then he's going to get worse.

George doesn't get a whole lot of help from his friends. They accept his sickness as health and, for the most part, encourage him to do nothing about it. Why???

Well, if they admit that George is sick they'll have to admit that they're sick too, for their behavior is very similar to George's behavior. For example, let's say that George drinks too much, or cheats on his wife. If his friends tell him that he's sick, that is, his drinking, or cheating is causing problems, or is wrong, then they'll have to look to their own behavior. So, they don't tell George that he's sick. He just has a cold, a cold in the head, everybody gets 'em they're common as sin.

The doctors in the story are any true friends, or spiritual guides. George didn't want to face them, because they'd call him to face himself. So he makes up all kinds of excuses for not seeing a doctor. And, of course, he dies.

In the original meditation, I then read Ezekiel 3:17-21. It's still a good idea.

5 — SAY IT AIN'T SO, SAY IT AIN'T SO!!

"How many?" "What ya got to offer?" These questions are, at times, most important to pastors who operate parishes, and to people who join them. For the pastor, *"How many?"* may focus on how many families are needed to make sure the parish survives? How many are required to begin a new parish. How many are necessary to insure that we can pay our bills? To quote a young lad of many years ago, *"Say it ain't so, Joe. Say it ain't so."* For the people, *"What ya got to offer?"* may focus on sports programs, the Mass times, or language. Do ya have programs for senior citizens, young adults? How about Day Care? To quote a young lad of many years ago, *"Say it ain't so, Joe. Say it ain't so."*

The quote, *"Say it ain't so, Joe. Say it ain't so."* refers to the 1919 World Series between the Chicago White Sox and Cincinnati Reds, and what's known as the Black Sox Scandal. The reason Chicago was called the Black Sox is a different story, and I'll not go into it. The quote comes from a disillusioned and disappointed young lad who accosted Shoeless Joe Jackson, one of the White Sox players who was charged with throwing the World Series.

I wonder if Paul, or John, would confront Christianity of our day with the same question as that young lad? Now, don't get the idea that I'm longing for a return to the good old days of early Christianity. Not at all!

The Acts of the Apostles tells me that, *"The Church was at peace. It was being built up and it walked in the fear of the Lord and with the consolation of the Holy Spirit it grew in numbers."* (Acts 9:31) If I want to know the peace the early Church had, I don't have to go back in time. That isn't possible anyway. I have to know this: *"If I want what they had, I should do what they did."*

What they did is not unique, or peculiar to any place or time. The peace they knew is not the peace for which the world is endlessly searching. The communities they established, the parishes, had arguments and disagreements about the care of widows and orphans, about money, about the distribution of food, and many responsibilities. But, never-the-less the Church was at peace.

What'd they do to know this peace? I'd say they set priorities. They set them right and firm. I'd say they kept the "main thing as the main thing." I don't think they did this in a self-righteous unbending way, for they were often and abundantly the beneficiaries of compassion and forgiveness.

What was the main thing for Paul? Listen to his own words: *"Jews demand signs and Greeks look for wisdom, but we proclaim Christ crucified."* (I Cor. 1:22-23); *"I resolved to know nothing while I was with you except Jesus Christ and him crucified."* (I Cor. 2:2); *"But may I never boast except in the cross of our Lord Jesus Christ, through which the world has been crucified to me, and I to the world."* (Gal. 6:14)

Now, signs and wisdom are okay, but Paul insisted on keeping the main thing as the main thing, and the Church knew peace. The peace of being focused on Christ, and him crucified. Had he not done so in word and deed, surely there would have been someone to accost him with, *"Say it ain't so Paul. Say it ain't so."*

What was the main thing for John as he wrote to the seven Churches in what has become known as the Book of Revelation, or The Apocalypse? As I understand it, the main thing was, "The world may seem to be winning, and all may seem lost, but hang in there, cause Christ has overcome the world."

Now commerce and power are okay, but John insisted on keeping the main thing as the main thing, and the Church knew peace. The peace of knowing that Christ had overcome the world. Had he not done so in word and deed, surely there would have been someone to accost him with, *"Say it ain't so John. Say it ain't so."*

Today, I face the same problems as Paul and John — we all do. The world has changed, but the main thing hasn't. Numbers and membership are important, and so are sports, Mass times, language, day care, young adults, and senior citizens. But the main thing is still — *a crucified Christ has overcome the world*. The struggle, today, is the same as always — to keep the main thing as the main thing, in word and deed. If I don't, surely someone, perhaps a little child, will accost me, either here, or hereafter, with, *"Say it ain't so Bill. Say it ain't so."*

6 — IF A TREE FELL IN THE FOREST

There's a question that used to be very popular, with philosophers — "If a tree fell in the forest, but there was no one to hear the sound, would it make any noise?"

The question supposes that sound, like beauty, is within the ears or the eyes of the beholder. I think there's something wrong, very wrong, with the thinking that says there is no sound unless it's heard, and that beauty exists only in the eye of the beholder.

Does the beauty of God depend on the recognition of others to be real? I think not. All creation reflects the beauty of God. When we fail to hear or see it, we're the poorer — not creation, or God.

Jesse Jackson came out with a saying, "I am somebody." It meant that by the simple fact that a person exists they are somebody, somebody of worth and dignity. Before a person ever accomplishes anything, before a person makes a "mark" in society that person is somebody.

I think what Jesse knew was that in order for a person to make a "mark", to accomplish something, he or she first had to know that he or she is **SOMEBODY**. A "NOBODY" never did anything.

What I hear in the society in which I live is, "I'm a nobody until I do something." The message I hear is, "When you do something worth something, I'll recognize you as worth something."

I'm here to say, "I believe that when a tree falls in the forest it's not necessary for me to be there for it to make a sound. It's not necessary for me to behold a person, place, or thing as beautiful in order for beauty to exist."

Beauty is there to behold and sounds are there to be heard. Because I do not behold or hear does not mean they have no reality. It does mean that I'm the poorer for being unaware. I'm also convinced that my poverty does not enrich those around me.

The God I believe in has never, even once, told me that I had to do something worthwhile, if I was gonna be worthy of His love. What God has told me, (in John's letters) is that it's not that I first loved God, but that God first loved me. I'm told in the Gospel, *"Are not two sparrows sold for next to nothing? Yet not one of them falls to the ground without your Father's knowledge. So do not be afraid; you are worth more than an entire flock of sparrows."* (Mt 10:29-31)

Father Richard Rhor asks, "Does God love me because I'm good, or am I good because God loves me?" If God loves me because I'm good, then I've earned God's love, God owes me, and that ain't possible.

As I understand God's word to me, I am to love others as God has loved me. That means that I should strive to love others, not for what they've done, but for who they are. They are children of God — my sisters and brothers.

I can not say, "Because I do not hear you, you have no pain. Because I do not see your beauty, you have no beauty." I can say, "Because I don't listen, your pain is greater," and "Because I do not appreciate your beauty I hide it even from you."

We — you and I — have need of each other. We help and hurt each other. Although beauty and sound exist without my knowledge, my awareness of God's reality enlarges both you and me.

It doesn't take a psychiatrist to tell me that, *'self image,"* is a problem for many. It seems almost a contradiction that while self image is the sum of what a person thinks of him/her self, unfortunately, it is usually rooted in what others think.

In *THE LAST MEDITATIONS OF ANTHONY DE MELLO,* in a section called, "Become Like Little Children," De Mello asks, "Is there anyone today in whose presence you can, simply and totally, be yourself, as nakedly open and innocent as a child?" I can count a few people, and that tells me how much my self image is influenced by others. How important, and freeing it is to know that my worth comes not from the opinions of others, but from the hand of God. And how very important it is for me to share this with others, if I love them.

7 — BECKY'S MOM & SERENITY

I was visiting friends in Nashville recently. The mother of my hostess, Becky, was very ill, and not expected to live much longer. Becky's mother is in her nineties, and, as the saying goes, "she has had a rich, full life."

"Rich," has little to do with money, and much to do with Godly blessings. For example Becky is her twelfth child. My! My! How the definition of "blessing" has changed in our world.

Becky was telling me about her mother one evening. We stood in the kitchen, and she reminisced about the closeness of their relationship. She thought, perhaps, because she was the youngest, because she was her mother's "baby" longer than any of the others, that a unique bond was nurtured.

Becky told me that any of her siblings could tell mama that she should go to the doctor, or even the hospital, and nothing would happen, but if Becky told her, she'd go.

I met Becky's mom a year or two ago when I was visiting for Thanksgiving. What a very charming lady. I felt that she took a liking to me immediately, and wondered what I had done to impress her. Becky explained it to me when she told me that her mom has children, grand children, and great grand children and she loves them all the same.

She pointed out that all these children were children of different generations, yet her mother loved them all. She said the styles of long hair, and ear rings for boys, or various fads that girls go through were no barrier to her love. She just has a way of letting each person she meets know that they were accepted and loved just the way they are.

As Becky was telling me all of this, I searched for something to say that would give her the peace and serenity for which she longed. I didn't want to interrupt, so I mentally catalogued a list of things that I thought I could say that would be helpful.

She looked at me with eyes that were wet with warning and said, "I know she's at peace with God. Her minister of 40 years was by to see her just the other day. I know she's suffering now. I know she won't get well. I know she's had a good life. I know I'm going to miss that closeness we've shared, I know that too, will pass." As she talked, the list of things she already knew grew longer, and the list of things that I thought I should tell her grew shorter.

Just before she finished, she completely destroyed my list, and taught me a beautiful lesson. A lesson I thought I had committed to memory long ago.

She finished by saying, "I know all those things, I'm just not ready to accept my mama dying."

In those words she recalled for me the lesson I had learned and forgotten. I wanted to comfort her, I wanted to give her peace, and serenity. I wanted to do all this by telling her things, by teaching her truths. I wanted to give her serenity through knowledge, she reminded me that serenity comes through acceptance, not knowledge.

So I did the only thing I could do, and it was the right thing to do. I gave her a hug. I held her tight. She coughed or maybe cried — I don't know. It's not important. What is important was the hug. It was such a simple thing, but it was the right thing.

I couldn't give her peace — or serenity — but I could give her a hug, and she could discover serenity, peace within herself in God's good time. Serenity is discovered through acceptance, and acceptance does not often come by way of facts and figures, but frequently does come in a simple embrace — a hug. A hug that says more fully than any fact, "I care."

If you ever wonder what you should say to a person who is suffering, or if you are just at a loss for words, remember that person probably already knows exactly what you are going to teach, or tell. So just give them a hug. Feeling, not just knowing, that someone cares is the beginning of acceptance, and acceptance is the road to serenity.

8 — WHY THE WEALTHY AREN'T HAPPY

In my meditation this morning there was a quote from Philip Slater. It read, *"One of the main reasons wealth makes people unhappy is that it gives them too much control over what they experience."* Even though I thought he was writing about material wealth, what he wrote seemed so totally around the bend that, although I didn't know him, I was sure he had to be out of his gourd. I was taught that my goal was to grow up, and be responsible. Now, to be responsible for what I do, I have to be in control. Right? So how can I have "too much control"? Something there just didn't ring true.

Then I remembered what a professor in college told me years ago. I was about to correct something he had said. I prefaced my remarks with, "I read a book that said..." He interrupted me with, "That's nice. Now go back and read another one." And he went on to answer my brilliant clarification before I even got a chance to make it.

So, back to this morning's meditation; I read the second sentence. "They try to translate their own fantasies into reality instead of tasting what reality, itself, has to offer." Well, "what's wrong with that," I thought, if people didn't try to translate their fantasies into reality, we'd never have gone much beyond the wheel. Kids would still be walking 12 miles to school through snow and storm, and I'd be writing my column by hand instead of on a computer. I was missing something that Philip Slater was trying to tell me. Maybe I'd better do what my professor told me — read and think a little more.

I'm coming to see that what he was trying to tell me was that, when wealth is used to avoid reality, rather than to cope with it, that's a short-sighted use of control, and the fruit it bears is tension, born of fear of loss, not happiness born of fulfillment.

I think this is true not only for those who misuse material wealth, but for those without material wealth who see it as the solution to all their problems.

I'm also coming to see that what he said was not necessarily limited to material wealth. I can misuse spiritual wealth. For me the acts of thinking, willing, dreaming, desiring are examples of spiritual wealth. If I use them to avoid reality, rather than to cope with reality, then I am not letting my wealth — spiritual or material — bring me happiness.

This would be the very opposite of the Serenity Prayer: "GOD GRANT ME SERENITY TO ACCEPT THE THINGS I CAN NOT CHANGE." To accept reality as reality, not as I prefer it to be... I can change material things, and I can change my attitude about them. I can't really change other people. I might affect the way they act. I can't change them, but I can change my attitude about them.

The second part of the Serenity Prayer pleads, "GRANT ME COURAGE TO CHANGE THE THINGS THAT I CAN CHANGE." In my heart I know there is nothing I can change but me. If I read the Serenity Prayer correctly, I know that happiness is going to be mine through the appropriate use of the gifts of Serenity and Courage that God gives me. If I read Philip Slater right, then, wealth — and the desire for it — can be a serious obstacle to happiness. It gives me the illusion of happiness through control rather than the reality of happiness, through acceptance.

True happiness comes to me through acceptance of God's reality. That's why it's better for me to ask for serenity to accept the things I can not change, rather than wealth to change things I don't like. True happiness comes to me through change — spiritual growth — in myself. That's why it's better for me to ask for courage to change the things that I can rather than wealth to change the things I don't like.

Wealth gives me the illusion of power and control. It's not the a-mount of money, or material goods, it's my attitude toward wealth that forms the illusion. It's a strong illusion. One by which I'm too often taken in. So, it's important that when asking for serenity to accept the things I can not change, and for courage to change what I can, that I also ask for the wisdom to know the difference.

It's this wisdom that helps me make sense of what Philip Slater was trying to tell me.

9 — IF GOD'S SO GOOD, WHY'S EVERYTHING SO BAD?

Even in the midst of November, we can see the beauties of Fall. I've heard it said, and I'm sure you have too, "How can anyone, on seeing the beauties of nature: the leaves in the Fall; the flowers of Spring; the simplicity of the Rainbow; the majesty of the mountains, doubt that there is a God?"

It's a good question, but the flip side of it is, "How can anyone on seeing the ravages of nature: floods; drought; earthquake; avalanche, believe there is a God?"

A question I like to ask is, "On seeing the actions of people striving for unselfish love, can anyone doubt the existence of a loving God?"

But this question too, has a flip side. Some people ask, "How can anyone, in the midst of all the evils in the world: starvation; ethnic cleansing; racial hatreds; killing of the unborn; and on and on and on, believe there is a loving God?" Another question the skeptic poses is, "If God is all powerful, and in charge, why is everything going to hell in a hand basket?"

I remember asking questions like these when I was in the Air Force during the Korean War. The answers I found did not lead to a celebration of faith, but to a reveling in what Fr. Jay Jackson used to call, "My Pagan Days."

Things are somewhat different now. I still find the beauties of nature and the goodness of people to be magnets that attract me to the reality of God. But natural tragedies, and mankind's inhumanity to one another, though still repulsive and shocking, no longer repel me from the reality of God.

The change in the way I cope with evil came about as I began to discover some startling reactions to the evil of Adolph Hitler. *The Diary of Anne Frank* reveals a young girl who believed in the sun, even when it wasn't shining, and who believed in God even when she couldn't find Him. Maximillian Kolbe, the priest in the concentration camp, demonstrated a personal power and control when he laid down his life for another, in defiance of man's inhumanity to man. Dietrich Bonhoeffer, the theologian, seemingly without hope, in a Nazi prison, wrote of his conviction that something good would come from it and the power of those words is at work in our world even to this day.

Why these reactions in the midst of such horrors? Why? Because they believed in a Power Greater than the evil around them. In my "Pagan Days" I did too. But I wondered if He cared. If there was a Power greater than the evil of war, shouldn't that Power be in control?

My dilemma, as I see it now, was in my understanding of power and control. What does it mean, to have power? To be in control? Three more people, who, to all appearances had little power and less control, come to mind in answer to that question.

GANDHI stood unarmed against the British Empire. He told them to leave his country. They laughed, but in the end, they left. MARTIN LUTHER KING stood against racial injustice armed only with the power of conscience, and a Dream. They killed him, but conscience and the Dream live on. And finally, the POPE. As World War II neared its end, Churchill, the British leader, suggested to Stalin, the Russian dictator, that perhaps they should consult with the Pope. Stalin laughed and replied, "The Pope! How many divisions does he have?" Stalin and the communist empire have crumpled — the Pope and the Church live on, and the Pope still has no armed divisions.

There is a power greater than evil around us. It is not a sleeping power. It is not a power that does not care. There is a power greater than evil and that power is GOD.

So very often we conclude our prayers with, "one God, Who lives and reigns forever." Where does this powerful God live, and how is His control felt? Not in the strength of military might, nor in the coercion of global economics. The power of God, and His control is to be found in the hearts of those whose faith lives beyond the test of time and patience, and in unselfish acts of love of neighbor.

The Skeptic will doubt, and the cynic will deride, but experience is proving, to those open to proof, that faith, hope, and love bring more serenity than all the arms and all the armies the world has ever known.

10 — IT PAYS TO ADVERTISE

I have often heard the saying, "Beauty is in the eye of the beholder." Perhaps you have too. I most often hear it from people, who for their own reasons, seek to deny the reality of objective beauty. I kinda think that it's a put down, even though it pretends to respect, or at least, acknowledge my right, or my ability to see beauty where others do not.

There are people, and have been for a long, long time, who seek to convince everyone that there's only one kind of real beauty. They've been pretty successful at it, too — they've made a ton or two of money from it.

Now I don't begrudge any particular industry the right to make a living — and to be of service to its customers — and I have no problems with businesses that just do straight forward advertising. But I'd like to know what gives a commercial concern the right to classify "age spots" as ugly, to say that wrinkles are unsightly, or that gray hair is unacceptable.

Of course the industry will reply, "We're just meeting the demands of our customers. When we advertise, we're just informing the public of what we have for sale" — Bull!!

I've often thought, and I'm 'bout convinced that a company, with the right advertising, could make a pile of money offering for sale a cream that would produce those "enchantingly beautiful age spots," or those, "wondrous wrinkles of wisdom."

I'm a confirmed cynic, when it comes to S-O-M-E advertising. I enjoy being informed about sales, and new products, but I'm convinced that too often advertising is creating needs, not meeting them. I'm not saying they're to be faulted for that. As Jesus might say, "If the children of the Kingdom were as good at their job as the children of this world are at their's we'd have a much better place to raise kids." (ref. Luke 16:8 - The Dishonest Servant)

I want to get to the Children of the Kingdom, and encourage them to do their job, in discovering and advertising the presence of God in our midst. In a little book I wrote, called *"SIMPLY SPIRITUAL"* I pointed out that the only place that God is, is in REALITY.

I don't have any difficulty in finding God in realities that I think are beautiful. But don't you see where this leads: "This is beautiful, so God must be here." What I've got to do, is turn that around: "God is here, so this must be beautiful."

BUT, how do I know that God is here? Ah! Back to *SIMPLY SPIRITUAL,* The only place that God is, is in REALITY. Can God be present in the distended, swollen bellies of starving people? In the tragic lust for power that consumes so many lives? In the awful hatreds that are Ethnic Cleansing and Racism? Is God present in the reality of youthful homelessness, or the hopelessness of the elderly?

Of course God is present in all of those situations, if they're real - AND THEY ARE. Was God present in Jesus when He was condemned? When He was scourged, mocked, spat upon, and crowned with thorns? Was God present in Jesus when He was deserted by all, and suffered the shame of the cross? Certainly.

But was there beauty there? Of course there was. Not the feel good, taste good, looking good, nor "I like it" kind of beauty. But the beauty that's truth. The beauty of God that will not permit me to accept misery and suffering as the norm. A beauty that alerts me to awareness of the goodness for which God has made us, and to which He calls us.

There is a beauty in suffering humanity. The beauty that called Francis to kiss the leper, and Mother Teresa to embrace the dying, and the homeless. There is violence on the streets that claims the lives of children. This is real, so God is there, and so is beauty.

It is a beauty that calls Francis, Teresa, Martin de Porres, and all of us to go beyond the suffering, ugly Christ, and bring about a Rising, beautiful Christ, and to know that they are one and the same. Is it possible that this insight could begin with the small reality of seeing beauty in age spots, wrinkles, and gray hair? For me it is.

11 — WHERE DO OBLIGATIONS COME FROM?

Christmas is, for many of us, a time for remembering. My Christmas memories are pleasant, sad, and even unusual.

The pleasant ones are from my childhood, and my days of a maturing spirituality which have enabled me to be more in touch with the "Reason for the Season." My sad memories find their origin in those first few times I was away from home. The unusual memories are rooted in the time before I began to be aware of my own spiritual responsibility to celebrate Christmas.

It's the unusual ones that I write about today. These I built while I was a C & E (Christmas and Easter) Catholic. I was in the Air Force then. Away from the authority of my father, the coercion of my pastor, and the customs of my family. I was the "original angry young man" joining the ranks of thousands of other "original angry young men."

The very idea of anyone telling me that there was an obligation to (or I "had to") go to Mass on certain days just rubbed me the wrong way. As I saw it, there was a lot more spirituality in going to Mass because I wanted to, instead of because I "had to."

Even to this day when I do something nice for someone and they respond, "You don't have to do that." I usually say, "I know. I enjoy doing it, but if I had to, I probably wouldn't do it." I suppose this attitude is a residue of my "angry young man" days when I resented obligations in particular and law in general.

I've made some startling discoveries over the years about Church Law. I was surprised to learn that the major purposes of Church Law are to protect the rights of members of the Church, and point to pre-existing obligations — not to create them. Now that's a concept that was entirely alien to me. How can there be an obligation without a law?

Remember when the lawyer asked Jesus, "Teacher, which commandment in the law is the greatest?" (Mt 22:36) And, of course, the answer was that we should love God with our whole heart, etc. and our neighbor as ourselves. Now tell me, did the obligation to love God and neighbor begin with the law, or did the law simply point out an obligation that we already had?

Obligations come, not from laws, but from relationships. Take the law God gave His people about keeping holy the Sabbath. It was for His people, because they were in relationship to Him. The obligation was already there in principle because of the relationship. The law brought it out of the abstract and made it concrete.

For God's people, who accepted Jesus as the Messiah, the day of the resurrection was more appropriately the Lord's Day. For this reason the early Christians gathered on the first day of the week for the "Breaking of the Bread," what we now call the Mass. The keenness with which they felt this obligation, or responsibility, was demonstrated in their willingness to risk their lives to come together. Later the Church used a law to point to this pre-existing obligation.

A spouse, a parent, or a child may, or may not, remember a wedding anniversary, or birthday. There's no law requiring a spouse, a parent, or a child to remember such dates, but is there a spouse, a parent, or a child alive who doubts there's an obligation?

I was a C & E Catholic for a few years when I was young. I didn't like the Church telling me I couldn't do this, and I had to do that. Those were just man-made laws anyway. I wanted to be free. God made me to be free. Didn't He? So why all those laws?

I'm coming to realize that, most often, obligations come from relationships, not laws. I'm in relationship with God, that means obligations. God's gonna love me, cause God is love. God's gonna be faithful to His Word, cause God is faithful. One might call that a supernatural obligation. It's not just God and me, it's God and US. It's US as the human race, US as the Body of Christ, and that means obligations, between God, and me, and us, and between us and us.

Church laws still irritate me, now and then, but that's alright as long as I remember that I'm part of the family, the Body of Christ, which is the Church.

12 — MAGY'S CHRISTMAS STORY

I want to share a story with you. It's about the strange ways that God works in a person's life. It was passed on to me some years ago by Magy. I lost the copy of her story and have reported it with some of the facts mixed up. Recently Magy helped me correct some my major mistakes.

It was fifteen days before Christmas. Magy was angry, and in no mood to celebrate the joy of the season. She and her father lived together. They had reasons to recall happy memories of Christmas with Charlie, Tommy, Bill, and Bob, her brothers, and Rosemary, Micki, and Kannie, her sisters.

Magy remembered family traditions, especially the Nativity scene. She and her brothers and sisters would vie with each other year after year to see who could put up the most realistic display. The scene changed from year to year, but the figures remained the same. A piece would be broken now and then. The figure would be repaired, but never replaced. These were happy memories, but this year they didn't move Magy. She was angry and Christmas made no difference.

It might help if you knew why. It started that first week in December. A accident took the life of her brother, Tommy. Returning from the funeral she thought, "How incongruous - Christmas decoration and grief, DEATH AND CHRISTMAS!!" She had to accept Tommy's death. There was no choice, but there was a choice with Christmas.

She numbered each day to see how quickly Christmas would disappear. The rest of the world could prepare and decorate, but she'd have none of it. Her decision was final and firm. There'd be no Nativity Scene, either.

Her father said little until two days before Christmas. That evening he brought out a box of old snapshots. He searched until he found that photo of that special Nativity scene. The one fifteen years ago. The one that everyone in the family had said was the greatest. He looked up at Magy and asked if she knew why the Nativity scene was such a special family tradition.

Magy stumbled for an answer, but her father continued. The familiar authoritarian figurehead disappeared, and she was able to see him as a person filled with sensitivity and dignity.

Her dad spoke of a son, a brother she'd never known. She'd seen pictures. She knew he was her parent's first born. He was Sidney Jacob, Jr., and she recalled his nick-name, "Little Daddy." She knew he had been hit and killed by an automobile when he was five. Her father told her what she didn't know. Little Daddy had been killed as he ran across the street to greet Santa. He had been buried on December 23rd. Her parents had other children at home. None old enough to understand death, but most were old enough to anticipate the joys and happiness of Christmas. So it was with the simplicity of a small Nativity set that her parents met the challenge of Death and Christmas.

Her dad showed her the picture of the Nativity scene taken when she was twelve. A cow's leg was missing, the face of the camel chipped. She studied the picture and remembered her father keeping watch over the Nativity scene each year of her childhood. For the first time since Tommy's death she slept.

The next day Magy avoided the Christmas party where she worked. She hurried to the Christmas tree lot where pickings were slim, but adequate. At home she found the Nativity figures hidden away in the garage. While her father prepared the evening meal she prepared the Nativity scene.

Many pieces had been repaired since that picture, but none replaced. She set each figure with great care. The three Kings with their camels came in from the east. The sheep and shepherds were on the opposite side. The donkey and cow rested on Spanish moss in the stable with Mary, Joseph, and empty manger to be filled at mid-night. Angels were hung on pine branches, and the Star of Bethlehem shone from the highest point.

When her father came in with dinner he saw and approved. That evening they shared many happy memories. The anger caused by grief disappeared, and Tommy's name was spoken without pain.

This story's true — I know. Her dad is my dad too and Magy's my sister. She sent me the story at Christmas time. It was the third year after my Bishop had charged me with the job of starting a new parish. It was not growing as fast as had been anticipated, and discouragement was an unpleasant taste to me and my people. I shared this story with them, and we all took new courage. By the way, the Bishop had named the parish before I was assigned. He called it the Church of the Nativity. God works in strange ways in my life and yours, too.

13 — MEEKNESS AND HUMILITY!! — AS A SOLUTION?

Violence seems to be the very hallmark of our day. Its use as a quick and easy solution to the very complex problems of relationships is clearly a failure, yet it's always at hand. The search for a suitable substitute often ends up in verbal, if not physical violence, and has everybody talking at once. I find the solutions offered by this cacophony of voices to be so confusing that I hesitate to add to it. Never-the-less, I'm convinced that what I have to offer is worth the risk.

What I have to offer is not original. What I have to offer has been tried before. Most of those who have tired it have found it lacking, and discarded it. But there are those rare few, who not only tried it, but accepted it as a way of life, and they have found it more than adequate for their needs. I speak of Gandhi and King, of St. Francis of Assisi and Mother Teresa of Calcutta. There are more of whom I could speak, but these will do.

What was their alternative to violence as a solution to problems? The question can be answered in various ways, I'm sure, but it always includes: **MEEKNESS** and **HUMILITY.**

The cynic this will say, *"Well of course, he's gotta say that — he's a priest. Priests are supposed to say things like that, but does he really think it'll work? Besides, what's he know about the real world?"*

I think the reason **MEEKNESS** and **HUMILITY** are so quickly, and almost universally, rejected as a means of solving problems is the way they are understood, or should I say *mis*understood, by the world. Unless I'm mistaken the two terms are usually associated with words, like *wimp, milktoast,* and *sissy.*

For the *New World Dictionary* Meek is: patient and mild, not inclined to anger or resentment. The *American Heritage Dictionary* has: Showing patience and humility; long suffering. Both of them list as the second definition: Easily imposed upon.

What does the scripture mean by Meek? I know neither Greek, nor Hebrew so I consulted the *Dictionary of Biblical Theology*, edited by Xavier Leon-Dufour. This began by quoting Matthew 11:29, *"Learn of me, for I am meek and humble of heart."* Jesus doesn't strike me as a "wimp." It went on to point our that Moses is the: "model of true meekness, which is not weakness, but humble submission to God, based on trust in His love. Meekness is the fruit of the Spirit, and the sign of the presence of wisdom from on high."

Meekness is as far from weakness as a ballet dancer, in top form, is from being out of good physical shape. Meekness requires a growing desire, and ability, rooted in a Grace-inspired trust in God to stand firmly against evil, and do it without resorting to anger, or resentment.

Humility is also *mis*understood. There's the sternness of steel about it, because truth is the core of real humility. Humility is not the denial of strengths, of gifts, or talents, but the acknowledgment of them, and of God as source of them. Humility is not wallowing in weakness, but an acceptance of weaknesses strengthened by a trust in God.

On the feast of the Holy Family, the *Commercial Appeal* published statistics on violence in Memphis. The scripture that day included Paul's Letter to the Colossians. It offered us a substitute for violence. "Because you are God's chosen ones, holy and beloved, clothe yourselves with heartfelt mercy, with kindness, **HUMILITY, MEEKNESS**, and patience. Bear with one another; forgive whatever grievances you have against one another. Forgive as the Lord has forgiven you."

Some will say, "That's *Church* language, it won't survive on the streets." But I tell you, it's the only real way to deal with relationships. It prompted Dr. Martin Luther King to say, "When you hate us, we will love you." It enabled Gandhi to stand against Colonialism in India. It inspired St. Francis to kiss the leper. It's the power Mother Teresa used to compel the rich to care for the poor.

It's difficult for us, who are accustomed to power and control as ways to deal with relationships, to think of meekness and humility as a worthy substitute. In the spirit I know it's true, but the world easily draws me to its bosom. Temper gets the best of me, and patience lasts no longer than an ice cube in the desert. Twin temptations nag me: 1) [Discouragement] "You can't do it, might as well give up." 2) [Half truth] "You're just a hypocrite. You know you really want to knock his block off."

This is when I have to realize that non-violence is where I'm headed, not where I'm at. Humility and Meekness are guides that all too often I fail to listen to. That's a weakness I'm learning to entrust to God. But I find this encouraging: Jesus meekly went to his death, that is, He accepted death rather than embrace violence. And you know what? When they put Him in the grave, and rolled the stone in place, they thought they had finished with Him. They laughed to themselves as they thought, "It's not the meek who inherit the earth, but the earth who inters the meek." What do you think?

14 — WINNING ISN'T EVERYTHING, IT'S...

"You win some, you lose some." This is often used by someone trying to console him or herself after losing a venture that was of the utmost importance before losing. It's also used to dismiss the importance of winning or losing. As I write this the Super Bowl is coming up. I can't imagine the winner using these words, however, the loser might.

All of this reminds me of Co-Dependency. What has, "You win some, you lose some," got to do with Co-Dependency? Well, the way I see it, it has a lot to do with it. "CODEPENDENCY" has been defined as, "the need to obtain an inordinate amount of one's self image, respect, esteem, from the opinions of others." I've heard a lot of definitions for this term but this one seems to be about the best. However, I'd extend it to include those whose self image is too closely tied to the outcome of any venture, be it business, sports, scholastic, or whatever.

Since we're so close to the Super Bowl, perhaps it would not be out of line to use sports analogies. Grantland Rice, the great sportswriter of a few years ago, wrote, "When the One Great Scorer comes to write against your name, He marks — not that you won or lost — but how you played the game." Compare this to words often attributed to Vanderbilt coach, Red Sanders and the famed Green Bay coach, Vince Lombardi: "Winning isn't everything, it's the only thing."

I don't know about you, but I'll stick with Grantland Rice. An attitude that espouses "winning" as "the only thing," also promotes the attitude that the end justifies the means. That is, if the end, the objective, is noble enough, the nobility of the means really doesn't matter.

It's noble to have a six figure salary, so it's okay to do whatever it takes to get it. Including lying, stealing, cheating, and so on. It's noble, cool, to wear these shoes, or that jacket, so it's okay to do whatever it takes to get them. Including lying, stealing, cheating, and so on, even killing. And the question keeps coming up, — "Where do kids get these ideas?" Where do you think? — From role models who live out these ideas.

We, uh... I guess I ought to stick to the first person singular. I tell kids that it's wrong to lie, to steal, to cheat, to abuse ourselves or our neighbor, or use drugs, (including tobacco and alcohol). And yet, in reality, I'm frequently tempted to do all of these things. Fortunately, not all of them at the same time. If the temptations are successful, from the devil's point of view I have several options at that juncture.

I can use the Karl Menninger Option. Several years ago Dr. Menninger pointed out, in his book, *Whatever Happened to Sin?*, that I can simply make sin a matter of law, and then find a hundred ways around the law. I can use the Peer Pressure Option. "Everybody's doing it. It must be okay." There's also the option that's currently in vogue: "Anything that feels this good can't be all that bad." I could use the Dostoevski Option. In his book, *The Brothers Karamazov* he suggests that one can avoid sin by abandoning conscience to authority figures, especially those in the Church. Then there is the Nazi Option of abandoning conscience to authority figures of the State. But conscience is like super glue. Once I come in contact with it, it's hard to let go. Finally, there's the King David Option, but this takes guts.

Remember King David? His army is off fighting a battle. He's walking on the roof of his palace when he spies, and is smitten by, Bathsheba. He has sex with her. When she conceives he goes for a cover up. He invites her husband to come home from the front and spend some time with his wife. When this fails he arranges to have him killed in battle. Nathan, the prophet, confronts him with his sin. All of the aforementioned options are open to him, but he goes for the King David Option — he simply says, "I have sinned against the Lord." (2 Sam. 12: 13)

Compare this with the story of Adam and Eve. God confronts them with their sin and they invent the, "It's Not My Fault" Option. Adam blames Eve and Eve blames the snake. From the beginning of our relationship with God we are drawn to a denial about sin. John, a friend of mine, shared an insight with me recently. When God came into the Garden after the sin, Adam and Eve were hiding. God asks, "Where are you?" (Gen. 3:9) What a strange question for God, Who knows everything, to ask. John's insight was that God asked the question, not for His knowledge, but that Adam and Eve might come to admit that they were hiding, that they were in denial about their sin.

Sin is losing. I've often found it so terribly difficult to admit that I'm losing, that I've lost, that I'm a loser. Even when cornered, when I've no choice, I'm tempted to say, "You win some, you lose some," in an attempt to dismiss the "agony of defeat."

There's another option. I call it the Pauline Option. It's all there in Romans 7:13-25. Paul says he can do no good on his own, but only in union with God. He says winning or losing is important, but only because winning and losing is determined by how I play the game. I was never meant to win by myself, and every time I try it, I lose. As a Catholic Christian I'm convinced that victory in the game of life means union with the Father. No one comes to the Father except through the Son.

So for me it can never be, "You win some, you lose some." For me, "Winning is the only thing," but as, Grantland Rice noted, the only way I can win is HOW I PLAY THE GAME.

15 — IT TAKES TWO HANDS TO HANDLE A WHOPPER

As I look back over more than a half a century of Lents, I discover that I've made some changes not only in the things I give up for Lent, but also the in WAY and the WHY I give things up for Lent.

I remember giving up SWEETS one year when I was a child. As soon as I made the commitment I discovered just how many things I'd been eating that were sweet. The next year I was more careful, and less ambitious, I just gave up deserts. The following year I was wiser still, and more precise, I only gave up candy.

I remember reading stories about some of the saints, and the penances they endured in order to grow closer to God. They fasted, lived in the desert, and some even wore hair shirts. I'm not sure just what 'hair shirts' were, but I don't think they were comfortable. There were even saints who endured the pain of rocks in their shoes. There were also saints of old who scourged themselves with cords.

When I was young I tried the pebble in my shoe, but quickly found that wasn't for me. I never got into scourging myself. As I look back on it, when I tried any of those physical penances, I always ended up with a Gordon Liddy attitude. Liddy would hold his hand over a flaming candle just to prove he could do it. It was a macho thing.

When I was a teenager there was always someone who would ask, "What ya giving up for Lent?" If it was a teacher, or the priest, or my dad, I'd give my answer, and then wait for some sign of approval. Man, how I hated it when all I got was, "Ha! Is that it? You're not gonna get much outta Lent if that's all you do."

If it was a classmate, we'd usually get into one of those, "Anything you can do I can do better," type of arguments. And I'd end up with more penance than I could do in one Lent, and certainly more than I intended to do.

I look at Lent differently now, and the view's great. The road I've traveled to get this view is simply what it took for me to get here. It is not a race, or a competition. I don't have to prove anything to anybody. I see the Church offering to each of us a common opportunity called Lent. It's a road to Calvary and as the song says, "We have to walk it by ourselves."

There's a journey through Lent that's common to us all, but the road I travel through this Lent has been prepared just for me by my God. I shouldn't follow anyone else's path, nor should they follow mine, but we can share with each other.

My journey through Lent is a journey to union with God. When I "give up" something for Lent, I've to come to see it not so much as giving up something, but as grabbing hold of something — something that will bring me closer to my God. An example I enjoy is the set of training wheels on a child's bike. If a child is never able give up training wheels, the child will never grab hold of the freedom that a bike can provide. When I give up something for Lent now, I expect more than just the pain of letting go of something I enjoy.

The pain of letting go all too often keeps me from letting go. The more real the pleasure of new life, the joy of discovery that comes from my awareness of God's union with me, and mine with Him, the more willing I become to let go.

I've made a discovery about living. The things that I enjoy— the things that I get a lot of pleasure out of — seem to be designed to lead me to a desire for, and a discovery of, greater joys just around the bend. The more real this becomes for me the more willing I am to let go of what yesterday seemed to be a source of permanent joy, fun, pleasure.

Of course there's a leap of faith there, there's risk there. That's what Lent's becoming for me, not simply a time to give up something, though that still remains, but a time to risk, to leap in faith. A time to say, "I enjoy this, but I trust my God. I dare to risk that my God has something even greater in store for me. But first I gotta let go of this, so I can grab hold of that. What I'm being offered is the Kingdom, in a whole new way. But I can't hold on to today's dead sanctities with one hand, and grab The Kingdom with the other. Why? Because, to co-opt the people at BurgerKing, "The Kingdom of God is like a Whopper, and it takes two hands to handle a Whopper."

16 — THE PARKING PLACE

Driving to a shopping mall, last week I said to a friend, "You just watch, the only parking place will be miles away." As I said it, I remembered I was going to try to give up being negative.

Against all odds, and without waiting or driving around, I found a parking place not 50 feet from the entrance. That incident is very valuable to me now. Every time I catch myself being negative I say, "Remember that parking place at the mall."

There have been times when I've said, "What's wrong with being negative? At least that way I'm never disappointed, and I'm always pleasantly surprised when things go right." These times come and go, so I'm sure that attitude will hit me again. But what's wrong with it? Seems like a perfect way to avoid disappointment, and guarantee serenity. There **is** something wrong with it, and when I take the time to think it through, I can see it.

Maybe it's just joking around. Maybe it's just about little things, things like parking places. I can't speak for you, but with me little things have a way of growing. They have an insidious way of forming an attitude before I'm even aware of it. As one person told me, "An ounce is not very much, but you can't have a ton without it."

Alright, so it builds an attitude that can govern my life. So what's wrong with that as long as it avoids the pain of disappointment and guarantees serenity?

When I'm in one of those moods, it seems the only way I can look at life is in extremes. Life is either negative or positive.

Like the guy said, "I've been rich and I've been poor. Rich is better." If that's all there is to life, I'd have to agree, but life is more than rich and poor, more than sick and well, more than happy and sad — LIFE IS REAL!!!

A negative attitude reminds me of a German philosopher, of many years ago. He looked at life as a bed of hot coals with a cool spot now and then. He expected little out of life, and I suspect he got little from it. I don't know if he believed in God, but I couldn't believe in any kind of god he'd come up with.

For me a negative attitude has only one destination — HOPELESSNESS. For several years I was trapped in an addiction which was fertile ground for a negative attitude. I can tell you that negativity leads to HOPELESSNESS, even when that negativity is limited to only a few areas of one's life — or to just one. I remember one time telling a friend how happy I was when something turned out well. I said, "Things don't usually turn out that way for me, but that's alright, cause I don't expect things to turn out well."

His reply was most unexpected, "What's the matter? Don't you believe God loves you?"

"Well, yeah, but what's that got to do with it?"

He went on to tell me that if I really believed that God loved me I'd expect good things. He said that because I expected bad things, because I had a negative attitude, I was blinded to the many good things going on in my life that were evidence of God's love for me. And, of course, I said, "What good things." And he replied, long before Rush Limbaugh, "See, I told you so."

From that time on I began to ask myself, "What am I looking for in life? What makes an outcome good or bad?" I had to admit that I had compartmentalized my life. There was the

Spiritual and the material, and I thought I was very comfortable with that. It was in the material area that my negative attitude loomed large. Sure I'm made of body and soul, but I'm just one person. So I can't live a Spiritual life and a material life. I've only one life to live. I remember Jesus telling his apostles, "You must be in the world, but not of it." I'm coming to see this as meaning that my whole life, Spiritual and material must be governed by Spiritual principles, not material ones.

Someone told me, "I guess that means that you get your reward in heaven, but you suffer here." That's what it meant for Karl Marx, but that's not what it means for me. The God I believe in loves me here and now. It's not some pie in the sky promise

When I try to live my life by Spiritual principles it doesn't mean that I'm free of pain, suffering, and disappointments. It means that I have a new way of looking at those occurrences which are common in everyone's life. Scott Peck says it very clearly in his book, *Further Along The Road Less Traveled*, "The quickest way to change your attitude toward pain is to accept the fact that everything that happens to us has been designed for our spiritual growth."

Spiritual Growth, growth to maturity, is a very satisfying experience for me. It has more to offer than any material growth, because it can always offer more. There's always more to be revealed. In material terms, it's something like golf — there's always room for improvement. When Scott Peck says "everything," does that mean that disasters and sin are good? As Paul said in his Letter to the Romans, "Of course not!" (Romans Ch. 7) It does mean that, dependent on my relationship with God, I can grow from them, and Growth, Spiritual Growth is a most enjoyable experience. It costs, of course, but it costs $10.00 to go to the movies — and they're not even real.

17 — THE LITTLE MAN UPON THE STAIR...

Howard gave me this little poem by Dorothy Parker the other day. I like it, and thought I would pass it on to you.

**"Last night I saw a man upon the stair.
A little man who wasn't there.
He wasn't there again today.
Oh Gee, I wish he'd go away."**

Who was the Man upon the stair? Why did he have to go, if he wasn't there? The Man upon the stair is sometimes big and sometimes small. Sometimes loud and sometimes quiet. He's sometimes quite troublesome, and sometimes just mischievous. He's always looking for an argument, and often, too often — for a man who isn't really there — he wins. He lives, and lives quite well anywhere he's accepted, but he dies, and dies quite quickly any time he's forced to tell the truth.

What's his name? He has no first name, nor middle either. His name — first, last, and middle — always is: FEAR.

Fear often claims kinship with caution, with prudence, but when the truth is known there's no kinship there at all. The only dignity fear has is that which it can steal from caution or prudence.

As I look back over my life many, if not most, of the things I've been afraid of never came to pass. As for the rest, all the rest, I'm still alive, so I survived them, and I've learned from them. I've learned different approaches to situations and problems, and even when I didn't learn I still survived. I've listen to the experiences of others and learned to apply what I need to my predicament.

But, you know something, the first thing that Little Man does, the one I saw upon the stair, that Little Man who wasn't there — the first thing he does — is cloud my memory so I forget all about past experiences, and then that Little Man leads me into delay, at best, and full stop, at worst.

If I'm ever to get rid of that little pest, I'm going to have to do more than wish him away. However, in a more realistic sense, I don't think I should try to be rid of fear, even of meaningless, unreasonable fear. For the breeding ground of fear is also the birthplace of prudence, and caution, and courage. I've found a better way to deal with that Man I saw upon the stair, the Little Man who wasn't there. It's called "coping." Since there seems to be no way of avoiding fear, I'd best learn to cope with it.

There are only two things about which I experience fear: 1) The Known, and 2) The Unknown. That covers a lot of territory, but I find there are ways of coping with both.

About The Known: If I know it, that means I survived it, so I begin with a plus. I've taken history, algebra, psychology, spelling, and many other kinds of tests. I've passed some, I failed some, but I'm still here, so I survived them. I've been through the extraction of wisdom teeth, migraine headaches, and gas. I wouldn't plan any of them for a vacation, but none of them came to stay, they only paid a visit.

The point is that in all of the unpleasant experiences I've had, fear was there to greet me, and fear always lied to me. Fear told me I couldn't survive failure, I couldn't endure pain, that the unpleasant experience I was facing would last a life time, and that I'd never be able to adapt to it. Fear told me something else too: "No one else will understand, so I must suffer this desert by myself." Experience tells me a great truth: FEAR IS A LIAR.

ABOUT THE UNKNOWN: The Little Man I saw upon the stair takes full advantage of the unknown. There's a natural uncertainty about not knowing, but fear need not rule the day. There are ways of coping. When I became a pastor for the first time, I didn't know if I would — or could — meet the needs of my people. I didn't and I can't — but God knew that when He called me. I've never been a parent, but I can imagine the fears that plague an expectant mother and father about the life of the child in the womb, about their fitness as parents. I can only share with them that God knew that before he called them to be parents.

When I pray for this or that, the outcome is unknown to me. When I look for ways to cope with the fear this invites, I am obliged to examine the way I pray. Jesus often compared our relationship with God to an invitation to a banquet. Prayer is our way of accepting the invitation. I gotta admit that sometimes when I accept the invitation, I want not only to set the menu, but also the guest list and seating arrangement as well. (The scripture says James and John did just that.) When I go to the Lord's dinner like that I invite the Little Man upon the stair to travel with me.

Coping with fear of the unknown is, for me, an expression of my trust in God. I'm not always at the top of the scale when it come to trust. But thanks be to God, when I falter, I have the saints of old, especially the martyrs who, while not models of perfect trust, are perfect models for us who strive to trust.

Does this get rid of the Little Man upon the stair? No, but it helps me live in peace with him.

18 — NOW IT'S UP TO YOU, GOD.

In tragedies or disasters — both serious and simple — I've frequently heard the expression, *"Well, we've done all we can do, now it's up to God."* The phrase has many variations and, I've used most of them.

I remember searching for my lost dog late one night. I looked all over the neighborhood without success. I waited at home, hoping that he would find his way home. I tried to sleep, but sleep wouldn't come. I recall very clearly saying, *"Alright, God, I've worn myself out, now it's in your hands."*

Finally I did get to sleep, and sure enough, my dog, Sam, came through his doggy door, jumped up on my bed and woke me up. You know I was happy, and grateful, and I offered a prayer of thanksgiving.

There's a lesson there. I didn't learn it then, but I'm beginning to now, so I'll share it with you.

Why is it that I had to exhaust all, or a lot, of my efforts before I could say, *"Alright God, it's in your hands."*? I don't know, but I'm finding that my experience is not unique.

Why is it that, I have to fail doing it my way before I'm even willing to try it *HIS WAY*? I don't know how to answer that question. Maybe the way I learn best is through failure.

Another question I am beginning to ask myself is: *"Why do I have such a difficult time turning things over to God?"* I think it has something to do with the "human condition." I'm convinced that it has little or nothing to do with age. I used to think of age the same way I did of money. The more money I had, the more important I was, and the more years I could count, the smarter I was. But there are a lot of people, older and younger than I, who can put things in God's hands a lot more quickly than I can. I'm also discovering that people, both rich and poor, have difficulty letting go of things. Much to my relief I'm coming to understand that union with God is not a competition.

Before I wander too far afield, let me narrow the focus a bit. I'm talking about the phrase, *"I've done all that I can do, now it's up to God,"* or some variation thereof. What's wrong with that? It sounds very pious, accepting God's place in my life, and all that. But what's wrong with it, is the word **NOW**.

It's like the child who wants to see what makes his dad's watch tick. He takes it apart and tries all day to put it back, and then says, *"I've done all I can do, now it's up to you, dad."* He should never have gotten into his dad's business in the first place. Or, perhaps, a better example would be a shift worker who wants to change shifts. He talks with everybody he knows trying to get them to change shifts, but without results. Finally he comes to the foreman, who makes out the work schedule, and says, *"Look, I've tried and tried, but I can't get anywhere with this shift change, from now on it's up to you."* The foreman, of course, replies, *"You should have come to me in the **first** place. That's my job, you know. Always has been."*

A Catholic tradition I'm familiar with is the "Morning Offering." In this prayer I place everything I do throughout the day in the Hands of God. This is a good practice. But it's somewhat like giving cold to ice, or heat to fire, or humidity to Memphis. By its nature ice is cold, and fire is hot, and Memphis is humid. And by God's nature everything is already in His Hands.

There's an *un*-intended arrogance in my action of placing this, or that in the Hands of God. It's already there. I could have known this from the meaning of the Divine Nature. I could have learned it from the song, *"He's Got The Whole World In His Hands"*. If, by using the Morning Offering, I come to realize this one, all important truth, then I'm doing more than just giving God something to do all day. I'm recognizing that I have a place in God's life, and not just that God has a place in mine.

As I sit here writing this, it seems like it's coming from an ivory tower. What does this mean to me for every day living? If I could grab hold of this thought, this principle, keep it, and live by it twenty-four hours a day, my life would be very, very different. I'd be free of many things: anxiety about my future; frustrations about my present; and concerns about my past. I'd never see the need to control, manipulate, or erase.

However, I'm like the tide, I'm in and out, I'm high and low. Anxieties, frustrations, and concerns will always be part of my life. From time to time, I'll seek to control, manipulate, and erase. I'll continue to place things in God's Hands, and still say, *"I've done all I can do, now it's up to You."*

But all that doesn't matter any more cause I saw once that everything is already in God's Hands, and that once is enough to keep calling me back each time I lose sight of it.

19 — WHAT'S HOLDING YOU BACK?

Someone recently put me on the spot with, "*People are suffering and dying in Rwanda, Bosnia, and Haiti, and you say the best way I can help is to grow in patience or self-control. How's that gonna help anybody? What kind of advice is that?*"

First of all, I'm not in the advice giving business. I don't write an advice column. I don't have any idea what anyone can do to help suffering people anywhere. What I write is a sharing column. I share with you what works for me. If it works for you we're both ahead. If what works for me doesn't work you, that's okay too.

Let me share this story with you. There were two Good Samaritans who really wanted to do something about the condition of the street people of the City. They both had an "in" with the Mayor, who had both the authority, and the answers for the problem. The Mayor, however, was a very busy person, and the Good Samaritans could only reach him by phone. But they had a problem. Although each of them had a phone, neither of them had a phone that was in good working order.

Each time a call was placed to the Mayor, there was so much static on the line that only a few words came through clearly. Each Samaritan had a different solution for problem.

Samaritan #1 decided to form a committee to work on solutions to the problem so he would be ready when he was able to contact the Mayor.

Samaritan #2 decided to work on the phone so that he could more quickly contact the Mayor and know what to do.

Both Samaritans knew that the solution to the problem of the homeless people could only be solved by contact with the Mayor. The way I see it, Samaritan #2 worked on the real problem. He didn't have any idea how to solve the problem of the homeless people of the City. He did know that the Mayor knew, so contact with the Mayor was his number one priority.

In the same way, I don't have any idea how to solve the problems in Rwanda, Bosnia, or Haiti. God knows. Perhaps God will give me the answer, perhaps not, but I'll never know for sure unless I make my number one priority the doing of what I can to be ready, willing, and able to hear what God has to say to me.

There have been many problems I've tried to solve without tending to my number one priority, or with just a hurried, or routine prayer. Every time my solution was tinged with motives of selfishness, power, control and a variety of other human weaknesses.

I'm beginning to discover that, the more I use God as a starting point, rather than a last resort, the more sound, workable, and acceptable are the solutions I discover.

Talking things over with God is a very personal thing for me. But the longer I live the more I realize that this holy practice has some built in hazards. It is fraught with temptations to use God to validate my own desires, and then to use this validation to, *"have it my way."*

At times like that I should bring into play something akin to the idea of Good Samaritan #1. I discuss the idea with other people. **NOT** with "Yes People", but with "Truth Speakers".

Consider this: I've never seen a commercial in which a sports figure testified to how much he, or she did **NOT** like the sponsor's product. Have you? That just doesn't happen with paid advertisements. When someone comes to me with the claim that their plan has been endorsed by God and needs no human scrutiny, I have reason to doubt that person's credibility. When I run into people who rush to accept such claims, I have reason to be amazed at their gullibility — even if it's me who's being gullible.

A lot of people share their experiences with me. For this I am very grateful. Some I find helpful, some I don't. All of it I find useful in one way or another. All of it bears the weight of human embroidery, the struggle to be honest, and just how honest to be. A lot of what I hear from others — not what they say, but what I hear — is but a mirror of myself. My weaknesses and my strengths, too. My tolerance and intolerance. My willingness to believe what I suspect is not true, and my stubborn resistance to acceptance of what I suspect is true.

I believe this experience of mine is simply part of being human. I also believe that every human tragedy, no matter how small or great, involves the weaknesses and strengths of the humans involved in it. So I think that if I work on the weaknesses and strengths of **THIS** human being, I have in no small way participated in the solving or preventing of some of the human tragedies that afflict this world.

There's a proverb that bears repeating here, *"Don't let what you can't do get in the way of what you can do."*

20 — WHY DOES GOD LOVE ME??

In the last several months I have encountered people who are convinced that they are going to hell when they die. I asked, *"Why on earth do you think that?"*

The reply shocked, and saddened me. It seems that they think that all the Church has preached is *"Hell fire and brimstone."*

Now, whether or not that's actually what the "Church" has been preaching is beside the point. If a person hears a sermon twice a year about finances those are often the ones he, or she, remembers. It wouldn't surprise me if the same is true about, *"fire and brimstone"* sermons.

It would do no good to refute the idea — based on the facts — of what the Church really teaches, though it is possible. One can argue as to whether or not the facts have been accurately interpreted. An argument can even be made about whether the feelings one has about these facts is justified. But there's just no arguing about whether or not one has feelings. And that seems to be the point.

Feelings are important, very important. As much as men like to proclaim they act on logic alone, my experience leads me to say, *"It ain't necessarily so."* Feelings are part of my life, but only a part of it, and that's why, *"If it feels good - do it,"* has never been a sufficient, or compelling reason to act for me.

If I had my druthers, I'd be able to believe that *"fire and brimstone"* sermons were a thing of the past, but I don't have my druthers. I have to acknowledge that *"fire and brimstone"* is still preached today, and I guess that there are Catholic preachers who share the burden. It sorta reminds me of what Jesus said about putting heavy burdens on the shoulders of people, and not lifting a finger to help in the carrying. (ref. Mt. 23-4 & Lk 11:46)

I'm aware that the preacher is the "Watchman for the House of the Lord." (ref. Ez. 33:2ff) I also know the duty of the Watchman is to warn, to protect, to lead and guide, but it's not to impose heavy burdens on people. Just as there are parents who introduce their children to the police (man or woman) by telling them, *"This is a policeman. Do what he tells you, or he'll put you in jail,"* so there are ministers who introduce people to God by telling them, *"This is God. Do what He says, or you can go to hell."*

One of the primary duties of the priest, if not THE primary duty, is to preach the Gospel. The word, "Gospel" means GOOD NEWS. As Father Rhor says, *"Not good advice, but GOOD NEWS."* I'd be hard pressed to say if there is one verse of the Good News that lights up my life more than any other, but this verse is pretty close: *"Fear not, little flock! It has pleased the Father to **GIVE** you the Kingdom."* (Luke 12:32)

Then someone said to me, *"Well, if it's all a gift, how come I have to keep all these commandments, and go to church all the time, and do this, and don't do that?"* When I hear that I'm reminded of the older brother in Jesus' Parable of the "Prodigal Son." He thought he deserved good things from his father because of all the things he did for him.

I find that often times people get our work ethic and secular economy all mixed up with the economy of salvation. The Parable of the Workers in the Vineyard has never set well with either Management or Labor. (Mt 20:1-16) They all got paid the same regardless of how long they had worked. I guess that's why it really is true that God's ways are not our ways.

Let me put this question to you. Who among you would feel good about your relationship with your son or daughter if he or she came to you and said, *"I washed and waxed the car. I cleaned the house from top to bottom. I did this and I did that. Now won't you love me?"* Wouldn't you try to tell them, *"Look, please try to understand. You're my daughter, you're my son — I already love you. You can do all these things because you love me, but not to earn my love.*" Father Rhor makes the same point with a different question. *"Does God love me because I'm good, or am I good because God loves me?"*

There are people who really think they're going to hell when they die. I think the stumbling block they encounter is a difficulty in seeing themselves as good people. They can't point to anything great and good they've done. Well, I have news for them, Good News. Remember St. Theresa — the Little Flower? She only did the little ordinary things of life, but she did them with great love. I'll tell you this too, I'm a Holy Man, and a Good Man, not because of what I do, but because of who I am. Not because I am God's priest, but simply because I'm God's child. And so are you.

21 — GOOD FENCES MAKE GOOD NEIGHBORS?

The other day I came across this idea in my morning meditation, *"There are two ways of spreading light: to be the candle or the mirror that receives it"* (Edith Wharton). I would have preferred, "the mirror reflects" rather than "receives," but in the meditation the sense is the same. It's a given that Light is to be shared, rather than owned — in the way that Love isn't Love til it's given away. Ms. Wharton was writing of love, of truth, not just light, but I'll call it Grace.

From her image many other images crowded my mind. Jesus, the Light entering darkness, and the darkness could not over come it. (John 1:5) The image in Genesis, ".. the earth was a formless wasteland, and darkness covered the abyss, ... God said let there be light." (Genesis. 1:2-3) The motto of the Christophers, "It is better to light one little candle, than to curse the darkness.

The essential characteristic, for being either candle or mirror, is to be OPEN, not only to share Grace, but to receive it. The Great Wall of China was built to prevent people from coming in. The Berlin Wall was built to keep people from going out. Both are monuments to futility. It's natural to be Open. It's easy for children, but difficult for adults. To be closed takes time and work. To become "unclosed" takes more time, and more work.

There's an often mis-applied quote from the Frost poem, *"Mending Wall,"* that some like to use to justify shutting in, or shutting out. The quote is, *"Good fences make good neighbors."* But the sum of the poem is caught in the opening line, *"Something there is, that doesn't love a wall."* The poem poses a perplexity and solves it, *"Before I built a wall, I'd ask to know what I was walling in or walling out, and to whom I was like to give offense."*

Another essential for spreading Grace, for being either candle or mirror, is WILLINGNESS. If I'm to spread the Grace within me, it's best I do it with a will, if it's to be of growth for me, or others. If I'm unwilling to spread the Grace within me, if I hold it tightly, I become like a Black Hole in space, sucking everything in and not letting even Grace escape. To be contained is contrary to the very nature of Grace.

The Lord has touched me with Grace. He's the candle. He's done so with a purpose spelled out in Isaiah, *"Just as from the heavens the rain and snow come down and do not return there till they have watered the earth, making it fertile and fruitful .... So shall my word be .... it shall not return to me void, but shall do my will, achieving the end for which I sent it."* (Is. 55:10-11) I'm the mirror. It is His set purpose that I not only receive Grace, but that I share it with others. I can only do that fully and completely if I do it WILLINGLY.

Grace is such a wondrously beautiful thing it's difficult to think I'd be unwilling to share it. When I see Grace as wondrous and beautiful, it's a joy to share, **BUT** it just doesn't happen like that all the time. Grace often comes to me in what I see as pain, failure, loneliness, betrayal, ugliness, weakness, sin — yes in the aftermath of sin. Grace comes to me when I've made a fool of myself, when I'm afraid to admit I'm wrong, when I don't get what I want. Yeah, Grace comes to me then, but I don't know it till next week. Even then I don't want to share it with anyone.

When it comes to the Grace I'd like to conceal, how do I let His Grace *"achieve the end for which He sent it,"*? How do I let it be fertile and fruitful? HOW, indeed? The answer is the **HOW** principle. I've mentioned **O**penness and **W**illingness. Now I come to **H**onesty. Together they form the *HOW* principle.

For me to bring Honesty to uncertain Grace is difficult. Theoretically I know that God is everywhere, or as Fr. Rhor says in *Quest for the Grail, "God is in all things waiting to speak and even to bless."* How can Honesty permit me to admit that God's Grace is in pain, loneliness, betrayal, etc.? Anne Frank wasn't lying when, while hiding from the Nazis, she believed in the sun, even when it wasn't shining on her and she believed in God, even when she couldn't see Him. Dr. Martin Luther King wasn't kidding when he told racists that when they hated him, he would love them. There is faith in the midst of doubt and love in the midst of hate. That's Grace in the midst of misery.

When I search for Grace in pain, loneliness, betrayal, etc., I do so honestly because God **IS** there. Not because of, but in spite of. When I reflect Grace in suffering it's not in a refusal to complain and it's not as a pseudo-martyr saying, "Look at me I'm suffering for the Lord." When I reflect Grace while suffering it's usually as a very unhappy camper, with a weak act of faith saying, "Lord, I don't know what's going on. I'm trying to trust You, and I know that this too will pass." That's faith, a weak, but growing faith. It takes Honesty to admit I don't like it, but with a weak faith I'll try to trust. I'll try to be Open to whatever I can discover of God's hiding places and I'll try to be Willing to accept what I can't change and to change what I can change, because God really is available to me at all times, good and bad, happy and sad. This is a goal of mine, not a task accomplished.

22 — DON'T SHOOT THE WOUNDED!

It seems to be a common practice when it comes to evacuation, abandoning ship, or a military retreat it's women and children first. However, there's a group that even takes precedence even over women and children, and that's the wounded. It's so obvious that it's seldom stated.

I remember the reports of what happened when the Khmer Rouge took Phnom Penh, the capitol of Cambodia. They needed hospital beds for their soldiers so they emptied them by kicking out the walking wounded and shooting the rest. When the Nazis rounded up the Jews, they would save the able bodied for slave labor, the others they would shoot or gas. Everyone recognizes how ghastly and inhuman this is. It's just not the sort of thing that good and decent people do to each other.

Just the other day I heard something that blew my mind. What I heard reminded me of a saying from childhood days. When someone would call me a name it always hurt, but the only solace I was given was fairly common at that time, and I guess it still is. I was told to repeat, *"Sticks and stones may break my bones, but names will never hurt me."* I used it, and I even taught others to use it.

But names *did* hurt. And I never knew why until that day someone blew my mind. It was an answer to the saying about *"Sticks and stones."* It went like this, *"Sticks and stones may break my bones, but names will break my heart."* That made sense. That was real. Names didn't break my bones, but they did hurt, and now I knew why. They hurt because I didn't understand the ignorance, or arrogance, or prejudice, or just plan meanness of those who were so insecure in themselves that they chose to bolster their self image by using names to bring others down to their level of insecurity.

Now that I know what the problem is, I'm learning to cope with the meanness of others because I know it springs from their woundedness. What that guy said the other night was like sunshine on a cloudy day, and it encourages me to continue in this coping process.

Remember, at the beginning of this column I told you how the Khmer Rouge, and the Nazis would shoot the wounded. I've heard that married couples, when they are really angry with each other, will throw zingers at old wounds. This is shooting the wounded. From personal experience I know that good friends, in the heat of an argument, can, and will do the same. This also is shooting the wounded.

Let me tell you where I heard that breath of fresh air that blew my mind. I was at a Twelve Step meeting. AA is where the Twelve Steps originated, but now-a-days there are Twelve Step Programs that serve many different needs. At most of these meetings chips, or tokens of various sorts are used to encourage the members to hang in there. They're used to acknowledge the accomplishment of short term goals. There's a white chip that's used as one begins the program, or begins it again. It's often embarrassing, even humiliating, to admit a slip, a failure, and to start again, but in recovery programs the White Chip is used to give recognition and encouragement.

The speaker at that meeting explained the White Chip in this manner, *"You know why we give White Chips, don't ya? We give White Chips because we don't shoot our wounded."*

I find that profound. From now on, every time I want to give up on someone, every time I want to declare someone incorrigible, or tell someone, *"This is your last chance,"* every time any of those things happens, I'm gonna tell myself, *"Look out, Bill, you're shooting the wounded."*

Someone is bound to tell me I'm letting them get away with murder. Well, I'm not. If they're getting away with murder, it's God who is letting them get away. Of course there'll be times when I have to let go, or surrender, but I'll let go, and surrender to God. If the way I live my life, the way I care, and have compassion seems to others that I'm letting them get away with murder, that's too bad, but I'm not gonna quit caring. I'm not gonna shoot the wounded.

There are many ways that I, as a Christian minister, can impose guilt trips on others — this too is shooting the wounded. But, if I pay attention to my "Book of Instructions," I'll know that I'm supposed to forgive others. Jesus tells Peter, not seven times, but *always*.

I'm supposed to forgive those who have wounded me, and those who are wounded. Lest I forget, this is a process, so I shouldn't grow discouraged, and give up. Discouragement is the weapon of choice for the devil. The next time I want to count somebody out, or give up on them, it'll take a lot for me to be able to blot out what I know is true for me: I'll be shooting my wounded.

23 — WHAT CAN I DO?

It was Thursday morning, January 5th, about 9:30. I stood in a small hospital room. It was crowded with a canvas carry-all bag loaded with paraphernalia for the new born, a fold-up bed for the young husband, and the regular hospital bed for the young mother who cuddled her first born son. Her husband looked at me with excited happiness, and pointing to the fold-up bed said, *"That's where I slept last night."*

"How ya doing, Debbie," I asked. She said she was a little tired, but her face, bathed with a smile of contentment that only a new mother would know, said much more than that. Sean told me how he'd cut the cord, and that he had been with his wife through the whole ordeal of labor and delivery.

Debbie offered to let me hold the baby, if I washed my hands. I've held many babies in my life. None have been so light, and meant so much. Sean spoke to his son, *"Ryan Patrick, this is your Uncle Bill."* There's no real blood relation between me and this family, but I've become very close to them over the years. Tears quickly began to blur my vision so I gave the child back to his mother.

It was Friday morning, January 6th, about 8:15. I was enjoying breakfast and the morning paper. The clash of realities and feelings from one day to the next could not have been more stark, nor painful. The *Commercial Appeal* carried a story from Chicago about an unwed teenager who, through fear of her parents, concealed her pregnancy, gave birth to her first born son in her bathroom, tossed the naked baby out a second-floor window into the bitter cold, and went off to school.

My first reaction was, *"How could a mother do that? How could anyone do that?"* Fear. Frustration. Anger. There ought to be a law. Ah, but there is a law.

After holding Debbie's and Sean's baby in my arms, not yet 24 hours old, I wanted to lash out, to erase this evil deed. But yesterday's horror is done — past, and can not be undone. *How could she have done such an evil thing?*

The paper said, *"The mother was very afraid of her parents."* The paper said fear drove her to conceal her pregnancy from her parents. Now understanding begins to be part of me, for I have been afraid before, very much afraid. I can remember hiding things from my parents, but never, never anything so very big, only little things. And then the words of the Lord Jesus begin to swell in my brain, *"If you can not be trusted in little things, who will trust you in great things?"* Yes, understanding begins to dawn, but understanding is understanding. It is not approval.

How can parents raise children who live in fear of them? I can hear people using this to justify children having abortions without parental knowledge, or consent. But this still does not answer the question of how parents can raise children who live in fear of them. Never having had any children, I don't know the answer to that, but in a world of children killing children and the casual acceptance of the term, *"sexually active teenagers,"* a euphemism for *sexual selfishness* at any age, compassion for parents begins to blossom. But compassion is compassion. It is not approval.

Robert Kennedy noted in his speech to the young people of South Africa so many years ago, *"There is evil in this world, and hatred, and starvation."* He pointed out that millions are lavished on armaments everywhere, and nations grow rich while people go homeless and hungry. So there is acceptance of the fact that there is evil in the world. But acceptance is acceptance. It is not approval.

Kennedy also posed a question in that speech, *"What can one person do against the enormous array of this world's ills — against misery, ignorance, injustice, and violence?"* That question is posed today. What can one person do when children are killing children? What can one person do when kids live in fear of parents, who live in fear of gangs, who live in fear of... ...?

The answer given then is valid now and always has been. Fear is an effective motivator, but it is not a healthy lover. Control gives birth to uniformity, but it does not give life to creativity. Change is what is needed. Not just change, but change that is growth.

If I seek to be an instrument of change, of peace, in a world that sorely needs it, I must begin with myself. I can not directly change the teenage girl in Chicago, nor can I directly change her parents. Laws are important, and needed. Rehabilitation and punishment have their value. But as President Bush had asserted, individual points of light are important, too. I look at the changes that have occurred in me, and I know most truly they've had their beginning, and nourishment in the seeds individuals planted and freely shared with me. So, if I seek to be an instrument of change, of peace, I must begin with me, not society, and freely give, what has been freely given to me.

24 — WHEN LOVE ISN'T LOVE

I'm reading *"Grace in Action"*, a book by a number of different writers, including Richard Rohr, a Franciscan priest. The first chapter, which was written by him is titled: "When Charity is not Love."

A point he makes is that while Charity and Justice should be distinguished, they shouldn't be separated. This is especially so when they are considered as Theological, or Godly virtues, and not just secular or governmental virtues. People still talk about Christendom and Christian Governments, but I agree with what Bishop Sheen said years ago — they don't exist any more, if they ever did. When I expect governments to be Christian — I tend to let them to fulfill my personal responsibilities as a Christian.

One of the things I enjoy about Richard is that, while he asks questions that make me think and makes statements that require me to look at myself, he avoids the political game of taking the side of the left or right. For example he says the vision of Christian Social Justice is not a vision of totalitarian equality nor is it capitalist competition.

He concludes with a quote from Cardinal Jaime Sin, of Manila: *"Strength without compassion is violence, compassion without justice is weakness, justice without love is totalitarianism, and charity without justice is **baloney**!"*

We've all heard the saying, *"Charity covers a multitude of sins."* Many are the times I've taken advantage of that. I don't claim to be in the top half of the class of sinners, but the saying has had its comforts for me.

I've heard about *unconditional love,* but I admit that I do usually get a warm fuzzy feeling when I get involved in works of charity. I'm encouraged by signs of gratitude, and seriously wonder how faithful I'd be to loving my neighbor without them. Most of the time I get more than I give — and I look forward that. These are encouragements for me. In some ways they are conditions that I set, and bonuses that I expect. *"How can this be unconditional love?"* I know God's the only One who can really love unconditionally. All I can do is walk in that direction, and that's good enough.

To get back to Cardinal Sin, it never occurred to me that justice without love is totalitarianism, and charity without justice is baloney. They are distinct, but if the Cardinal is right, and I think he is, then Charity and Justice are like the parallel rails that a train runs on. Each is whole and entire as a rail, but neither is complete without the other. As someone once noted, that'd be a heck of a way to run a railroad.

Many churches have Clothes Closets, Food Pantries, Soup Kitchens, Dinners for the hungry, and so on. Just when we begin to feel good about our charity, someone comes up with a guilt trip. *"If you care so much about the poor and the hungry you ought to do more about why they are poor and hungry, instead of just giving a meal and sweater."* Somebody else says it's better to teach people to fish than to give away fish.

I tried to solve the big problem one time. You know what I discovered? I discovered high blood pressure and ulcers. I discovered that the people I used to feed were going hungry. I also discovered that God gave each of us differing talents, so we couldn't argue about who was right, but we could work together to solve the problem. I think this is what Jesus was getting at when he stopped the *'beloved disciple'* who complained about, and wanted to stop those who were *'not of our company.'* (Luke 9:49)

I don't have a problem understanding love, even tough love. The world and the Church are pretty close on that. The world says love is living out the Golden Rule. I say it's trying to relate to others the way God relates to me.

But Justice, that's something else. The world measures justice in millimeters, and rules and laws. The Church values it as Grace. The world speaks of quantity, the Church of quality. When scripture speaks of one being *'justified'* I think it refers to being restored to what was lost through sin. I don't think it's talking about how correct I have been, but about Who I'm being made in the image and likeness of...

So when Richard Rohr and Cardinal Sin say, *"Justice without Love is totalitarianism, and Charity without Justice is baloney,"* what it means to me is that Justice is more than simply a measurement. It's restoring people to the image and likeness of God. And Charity, to be real, is a willing and joy filled participation in the work of Jesus Christ to restore all things to the Father.

25 — AT SCHOOL IN THE GUTTER

Recently I was at a meeting of ministers involved in Shelby County Interfaith (SCI). The meeting opened in the usual manner, with a Theological Reflection. This was led by Rev. Burton Carley, pastor of the Church of the River. With the intention of getting us to reflect on our own prejudices he used the Gospel of Matthew 15:21-28. The incident involves a Canaanite woman who pleads with Jesus to cure her daughter. Jesus ignores her, and when his disciples ask him to do something, he says, *"It is not right to take the food of sons and daughters and throw it to the dogs."* (Mt. 15:26)

Rev. Carley commented that if anyone of us were to refer to another as a *"dog"* that would certainly be grounds for us to be seen as prejudicial, and probably the subject of a law suit. He then asked us to recall events in our own lives that we could recognize as prejudicial. I recalled an event from my childhood. It was when I was very young, but it made a lasting impression on me.

There were five boys and four girls in my family at that time. We didn't have a car, and when Mom and Dad went shopping they would take the bus downtown to the A&P supermarket. On several occasions during the summer, my job was to start out walking with my red wagon, while my parents caught the bus. By the time I got to the A&P, the shopping had been completed. I'd load my wagon with groceries and start home, while my parents took the bus home. There was no difficulty to the job, and I felt good about being charged with this responsibility.

There was, however, a very scary part of the trip and this occurred both coming and going. At about half-way between our home and the A&P, there was a neighborhood where only black people lived. The area bore a name that, at the time, I found perfectly acceptable. I remember passing a school. It was called Douglas School. There was no grass in the school yard, and as a consequence, the school building was covered with a coat of dust, and it just looked "tired." As a matter of fact, most of the houses were covered with dust and peeling paint and the whole neighborhood looked "tired" to me.

For me it was a scary neighborhood — after all, I'd heard all sorts of stories about it. There were times when I wondered why it was like that, but I was just too scared to stop and ask, *"Why is this?"* One day as I was returning home from the store, I had trouble negotiating an uneven curb and my wagon turned over spilling the groceries in the street, in the gutter, and on the sidewalk. I was terrified. There were three or four guys (a few years older than I) sitting on a bench in front of a store drinking soda pop. I knew, without any doubt, that in a matter of seconds they'd be on top of me, and all the groceries would be gone.

I'd never, ever, stopped in that neighborhood for any reason at all. I knew better. But now, here I was standing dead still, not knowing what to do. I wanted to cry, but I couldn't. And I was right, you know. In a matter of seconds those boys were off that bench, and on top of all my groceries.

In a flash they had reloaded my wagon and helped me get it over the next curb. I was still frightened. I was confused, and embarrassed, too embarrassed to even say, *"Thank you."* Before I could realize what had happened, I was across the street, over the curb, and on the sidewalk. The four guys were back on the bench in front of the store with their sodas. I looked back only once, to see if they were following me. They just sat there, and smiled. They never said a word, and neither did I.

A lot happened to me that day. Lessons without words were both taught and learned. I don't remember telling anyone about it — I was afraid they would laugh at me. I've come to know that curb and gutter, that street and sidewalk, as one of my real "beginning places." I began to learn and unlearn some things there. A door was opened for me there, a door that has never closed — though from time to time I choose not to go through it. I began a journey there, a journey that I'm finding has no end, though from time to time I stumble, or seek to rest along the way.

Two lessons about my experience I'll share with you. These I began to learn that summer's day, so long ago. Fear is most often a liar. Contempt prior to investigation, or experience, is the home of the coward. I haven't learned these lessons perfectly. I don't guess I ever will, but I do make some progress now and then.

Fear and prejudice are stern and unforgiving task masters. They brook no liberty to those who serve them, and they grant no serenity to those who are their subjects.

Today I take my stand against them. Taking a stand certainly may not change the world, but as Father Rhor reminds me, it'll keep the world from changing me.

26 — HOW STRANGE — IT'S ORDINARY

I gave a talk on Easter afternoon five years ago on my personal spiritual growth. It was the first time I had ever done that. On Easter morning I was concerned about what I was gonna to say, and how I was gonna say it. At that time I was using, *Touchstones* a book of daily meditations for men. Each daily meditation was preceded by a quote from some notable person. Early that morning, worried about how I was going to do, I asked God for help. I opened my book to April 15th, and this quote from Hubert Humphrey jumped at me: *"Just be what you are, and speak from your guts and heart — it's all a man has."*

I was stunned, but reassured — God was still working in my life, even in the simplest ways. I know that God continues to work in my life, but I haven't changed a great deal — I still need to be reassured. This weekend, the Fifth Sunday of Lent, renewed that assurance. I shared this with my people in the sermon, and I thought I'd share it with you, especially since this will probably be in print in my column right after Easter.

In the first reading, Isaiah compares the return of God's People from captivity in Babylon to the Exodus from Egypt. But he tells them, *"Remember not the events of the past, the things of long ago consider not; See, I am doing something new!"* I decided to build my sermon around the point that God is still working in our lives today.

The other readings seemed to blend well. Paul wrote to the Philippians of his continuing growth in his relationship with *"My Lord Jesus Christ."* The gospel told the dramatic story of Jesus, the scribes & Pharisees, and the woman caught in adultery. Both told of God acting, not in the past, but in the contemporary lives of Paul, the Scribes & Pharisees, and the woman.

I shared with the people what Lerleen Thomas told me about her cataract surgery, *"Look what Jesus has done for me. I can see."* Lerleen was not claiming that Jesus had worked some extraordinary miracle in her life. She was acknowledging that Jesus is alive in her life through the ordinary skills of doctors.

I related two recent experiences of mine to the people. Late one Sunday evening I was called to St. Francis hospital to be with the Mascari family. Tony Mascari was seriously ill, and in danger of dying. I anointed him, and prayed with his family. I stayed with them as the doctor explained the situation. Finally I had to leave. I got lost trying to find my way out of the building. Suddenly a loud speaker urged the "Harvey Team" to report. I spotted a young doctor rushing through the hall in which I was lost. I was about to ask him how to get out of the building when he said, *"Come with me, Father. I'll show you a short cut."* He was too fast for me, but I soon found myself in the waiting room with the Mascari family, just before the news came that Tony had died. Ordinary events? Yes, but I see the hand of God there.

Then there was Billy, Billy Jolly. Years ago I hired Billy as the janitor at the Church of the Nativity. Even then he had trouble with his breathing. We became close friends, and after I left Nativity we remained close. We seldom talked of religion, he wasn't Catholic. He did prize his relationship with God, and we spoke of spiritual things from time to time. Some time back he lost the ability to talk.

When I returned from Tony's funeral there was a message that Billy was in the hospital and was not expected to live. Because of his pain he was on a morphine drip, and I thought might not know me.

I found Billy alert, and strong. I held his hand, and was surprised by the strength of his grip. We each knew that he was dying. I asked him if he was afraid. He shook his head, "Yes." Even though I knew he couldn't speak, I asked what he was worried about.

Then I asked, *"Do your sins worry you, Billy?"* He nodded a yes. I said, *"Billy, you're baptized aren't you?"* Another "Yes." Then Paul's letter to the Romans came to mind. I told him, *"Billy did you not know that all of us who are baptized are baptized into the death and rising of Jesus. Jesus came to forgive sins. Do you believe this?"* He nodded, "Yes". *"Billy, you know I'm a priest. I forgive sins."* Again he nodded. So I gave him absolution. He smiled a bit. I asked if he would like to hear some scripture. Another nod. You're probably not going to believe this, but I sang the 23rd Psalm for him. The way we do at Cursillo, but not quite as slow.

He smiled again, and I told him I had to go. I looked at him and said, *"Billy, the next time I see you, we will be in heaven. When you get there will you put in a good word for me?"* He nodded again.

Billy was buried on a Friday. I know what Isaiah meant. I don't have to remember the events of the past, or consider the things of long ago. I know God is still doing wondrous things in our midst. All this was in Saturday night's sermon.

Before Mass on Sunday, I read my meditation from Father Rohr's book, *Radical Grace*. The opening line was, *"Unless we can presume that the Lord is speaking right now, how can we believe that he ever spoke?"*

27 — I'M A CRACK(ED) POT

Today I write of a difficulty I have, and I think I have it in common with a lot of people. The difficulty is being able to acknowledge, to claim as my own, my weaknesses. Call them what you will — sins, bad judgments, mistakes. Whatever they are, I'm not comfortable with them.

A hundred years ago or so, when I was young and beginning to date, I worried about what to say to the girl I wanted to go out with. Suppose I said the wrong thing and she said "no"? I was afraid, but there was no way I could tell her that. Surely she would say no then. That was a weakness, but I am much older now, and things like that don't bother me. HA!!

· The particulars of events are different today, but I still feel the need to cover my weaknesses, my mistakes, bad judgments, sins, whatever. Let me give you an example. Say I have an appointment set for 2:00 pm on a Monday. It slips my mind. I get back to the rectory at 4:30 pm. The appointment has come and gone — angrily. Now what to do? Well, as far as I'm concerned, the best way to handle that is simply to call, tell them I forgot, and apologize.

There was a time when I would spend a lot of time and effort researching the facts (that is, concocting a story) so I could give them an explanation that'd be closely related to the truth, and yet not hurt their feelings. (That is, something that would save *me* from embarrassment.) Today I find it much simpler (but not easier) to just admit I forgot, make the apology, and go on from there. I've even come up with an idea that covers the situation when they reply, *"You forgot!!! I guess that means we're not that important to you." My response is, "Not true. The fault is not with your importance, but with me, and my memory."*

When I reflect on things like this it seems to be the rule that this human finds it difficult to declare my mistakes, bad judgments, etc., to anyone else. Ask the traffic cop that stopped me just how willingly I admitted I'd earned a speeding ticket. Ask my teachers of long ago how many different kinds of excuses I came up with for not having my homework. Ah yes, it's difficult to live with mistakes and bad judgments. The fact is that I frequently go to great lengths to cover them up.

Leaving judgments and mistakes aside, when it comes to weaknesses and sins I find there're a multitude of ways to avoid claiming my sinfulness. A few years ago Dr. Karl Menninger wrote a book **"Whatever Became of Sin?"** He says that one way we've dealt with sin is to make it against the law, and then find a dozen ways to get around the law. Another way I've observed is to call sin a virtue. For example some people opt for abortion, claiming to love children too much to bring them into this world of suffering and pain.

Liturgy and the Scripture present me with a unique way of dealing with my weaknesses and sins. On Holy Saturday night, in the Exsultet (the Easter Proclamation), the Church joyfully sings, *"O happy fault, O necessary sin of Adam, which gained for us so great a Redeemer!"* In Paul's Second Letter to the Corinthians he says, *"If I must boast, I will boast of the things that show my weakness. ..... (for the Lord has told me) 'My grace is sufficient for you, for power is made perfect in weakness.' I will gladly boast of my weaknesses, in order that the power of Christ may dwell with me."* (2 Cor. 11:30 & 12:9)

Recently I shared some insights with the young people at the Diocesan Youth Leadership Conference. I celebrated Mass with a small group on the feast of St. James, the Apostle.

The first reading, II Corinthians 4:7-15, told us, *"But we hold this treasure in earthen vessels, that the surpassing power may be of God and not from us."* The Light of Christ was the Treasure. That reminded me of a talk I heard a lady give on her personal spiritual growth. She claimed that the root of her spiritual growth was the fact that she was a crack pot, that is, a "cracked" pot.

She explained it this way: If, in a darkened room, a lighted candle is set inside a clay pot, and the top is put in place, and, there's enough oxygen for it to burn, will it give any light to those in the room?

Not unless there are cracks in the pot!!

She was speaking the same wisdom that Paul spoke of: If we know and claim our weaknesses, our sinfulness, we call attention to God's power, not ours. There's a lot of spiritual growth in knowing that I'm a crack pot, that is, a cracked pot.

28 — "TRUST ME," HE SAID.

"Trust me!" Now there's an invitation over used and abused. When the salesman or the politician looks me in the eye through the magic of television, and says, *"Trust me!"*, somehow I just don't really trust him, or her. Major events of the past years do little to encourage trust: A weeping mother pleading for the return of her babies, when she herself had killed them; A Witness publicly swearing to the truth of scornful lies; A prince and princess, icons of nobility, filling the tabloids and airways with acknowledgments of self-justifying adulterous affairs; Even men and women of the churches, going to jail leaving behind broken vows and broken trust. Is it any wonder then that the Good News - *that God does love us, and that we can trust the Father* — is seldom fully accepted at face value, so as to bring about changes in the way life is lived in this materialistic world?

In the last week of the Church year, the scripture for the daily Mass is taken from the Book of Daniel. The book is an early form of apocalyptic writing intent on giving a message of hope in times of dire stress. Nebuchadnezzar, King of Babylon, conquered Jerusalem and carried off to the land of Shinar the sacred vessels of the temple, along with some Israelites of royal blood. He intended to use these nobles in his court, so he fed them well. Daniel and his companions refused the king's food, insisted on vegetables and water, and thrived, much to the surprise of the King's chamberlain.

This was a testament, not to a vegetarian diet, but to trust in the Lord. The Book recounts the deeds of trust by Shadrach, Meshach, and Abednego in the fiery furnace. It tells of Daniel's trust in the lion's den. Luke tells us that we will undergo severe trials, even death, but we should not worry about a defense beforehand — we should trust Him. John says it's not possible to love God whom we do not see, if we do not love our neighbor whom we do see. This question may come up: If I can not trust my neighbor whom I do see, how can I trust God whom I do not see?

Some years ago I found an answer I'll pass on to you. The answer is Jesus Christ. But how does Jesus tell me that I can trust God? He goes beyond just telling — He shows me. I'd always understood that the suffering and death of Jesus opened the gates of heaven to us. This paid the price of our redemption. I never argued with that, nor did I fully understand it. Sure, there's mystery there, but there's also a lot to be understood, and misunderstood. One wrong idea makes the Father an ogre who is only willing to forgive sin if His Son suffers and dies.

To my mind there's no great gain in suffering, or dying. It's what I do while I'm suffering and dying that gives credit to them. It's what Daniel did. It's what the three young men in the fiery furnace did. It's what Jesus told us to do in Luke's gospel — trust — **TRUST THE FATHER**.

That's what Jesus did in the midst of suffering and dying — He trusted His Father. Oh yes, He cried out, "My God, my God, why have you forsaken me?" But these are simply the opening words of Psalm 22. It's natural to assume that the whole of the psalm was in His mind and heart. The psalm ends with these words, *"I will live for the Lord; my descendants will serve you. The generation to come will be told of the Lord, that they may proclaim to a people yet unborn **the deliverance you have brought.**"*

In the face of death on a cross, He trusted. *But, it was easy for Him, He was God.* Now, there's a cop out. Have you never read, or been told of what Paul, guided by the Spirit, told us? *"His state was divine, yet he did not cling to his equality with God but emptied himself to assume the condition of a slave and became as all men are."*(Ph2:6-7) The Church teaches that Jesus was truly God, and truly human at the same time. Paul says He emptied himself of the Divine prerogatives which means He knew human suffering and dying to the fullest. In the midst of that he also experienced human trust. It's His very human trust that tells us that we also can trust, and gives the power of healing and redeeming to His suffering, and to mine in union with His.

So, though the world gives me little reason for trust, the very human Jesus does give me good reason. He tells me, in the midst of all my failures, sins, and weaknesses, that He has overcome them all. When He says, *"Trust Me,"* I know I can. Not only that, He tells me that I should speak a word of hope and healing to murders, liars, and adulterers. It's important for them — and all of us — to know that the Father has not given up on us, that He wants us to trust Him, even in the midst of this bloody cross, in the midst of this world gone mad.

He trusted, but they killed him. And when they rolled the stone over the entrance of his grave they thought it was over. What do you think?

29 — NOBODY LIKES A 'DO GOODER'

The other day someone, in exasperation, asked me, *"Do you have to bring God into everything we talk about?"* That sorta stopped me cold in my tracks. I wondered if I had been coming on as a religious fanatic, or even worse: as a TV Evangelist. I was reminded of a warning Harry Sullivan gave me a few years back: *"Stop being such a 'Do-Gooder!'"* I thought one of the purposes of being a real part of the human race was to do good things, so I asked him what he meant. His response comes back to haunt me now and then. *"A 'Do-Gooder' is someone who is gonna impose his kind of good on you whether you like it or not."*

When I look again at the closing of Matthew's Gospel, I realize that the words were probably very carefully chosen. *"Go, therefore, and make disciples of all nations, baptizing them in the name of the Father, and of the Son, and of the Holy Spirit, teaching them to observe all that I have commanded you."* It's important I remember that the disciples were **not** told to *command* them to observe all that I have taught you, **but** to *teach* them to observe all that I have commanded you. In other words, Jesus did the commanding and disciples were to do the teaching.

Now, the way I understand things, all of us in the Church are disciples of the Lord. Although Bishops are the Official Teachers in the Body of Christ, all of us are disciples and bear some responsibility for teaching. How best to carry out that commission does present some problems.

For Deacons, Priests, and Bishops it should be fairly simple, for in the rite of ordination we are told to practice what we preach. But it's so much easier to command. Any parent who has ever dealt with a balky teenager knows that it's always easier to say, *"Because I said so, that's why."*

To get back to the original complaint: *"Do you have to bring God into everything we talk about?"* Well, actually I don't, because God is **already** in everything we talk about. In the world, He is usually hidden so there's a difficulty in knowing it. The question I've got to ask myself is: When I try to make that clear, am I commanding that you observe what I have been taught? Am I imposing my kind of goodness on you whether you want it or not? *"Vanity of vanities! All things are vanity!"* (Ecclesiastes 1:2)

If I'm gonna teach what I've been commanded, what's the best way to do it? How do I gauge success? I'm reminded of the old saying, *"The operation was a success, but the patient died."* I'm also reminded of the warning Fr. Rhor gave to those who preach the Gospel. It means, he said, "Good News," not good advice.

I'm discovering that the best way for me to teach is to consider the ways I've been taught most effectively. The best teachers I've had in my life are those who cared enough to share their experiences with me, not those who insisted I do it their way. Those who let me see how their values enriched their lives, and at the same time did not belittle what values I had. A teacher I greatly admire is John, the Baptizer, who said, *"He must increase and I must decrease."* (Jn. 3:30) This brings up the question: What am I doing? Building a reputation as a teacher? Or preparing the way for One greater than I?

I didn't set out to be a teacher. However, when I was a young priest I was assigned to teach in Knoxville Catholic High School, but it was quickly determined that that was the wrong assignment. Never-the-less, I am a disciple of the Lord Jesus, and therefore I teach. So are we all, and so we all teach.

I thought I'd share with you some of the things that work for me. To be a good teacher I must also be a good student. To be a good student I must know and live the **ROW** principle: that is, I must be *R*eady, *O*pen, and *W*illing to learn. I teach best when I share, rather than impose. I learn best when I respect rules and laws as guides in the formation of my conscience. I'm teacher and student when I honor the values of my life, rather than the thrill of the moment. I'm student and teacher when I let both failure and success be guiding lights, rather than blinding lights on the path I walk. It works best for me when I strive to be as patient with others as God is with me and when I don't take myself so seriously. Of course, these are goals I'm working on, not jobs I've finished with.

30 — BUT IN THE REAL WORLD...

Someone once told me that the journey to the Promised Land was more important than the Promised Land itself. It didn't make a great deal of sense then. I don't remember the reasoning behind the statement, but it had something to do with the descendants of Abraham becoming a people — a nation — on the trip from Egypt to the Promised Land. From Abraham to Egypt they were wandering nomads. From Egypt to the Exodus they were slaves. On the way to the Promised Land they became a people. They were growing up.

A friend of mine often uses this expression, *"I'm a growed up woman now."* She uses this when people try to slow her down, to tell her that she can't do this or that. I like the saying, but I object to the words, *"growed up."* I've no objection to poetic license and grammar's not the problem. It's the philosophy that bugs me.

Life's a journey. Faith tells me there's no end to life. There's no point in life where I can say, with any degree of finality, *"I'm a growed up person now."* There are some who will greet this with the same enthusiasm as Sisyphus. He was that character in Greek mythology who was condemned for eternity to push a stone to the top of a steep hill only to have it always roll down again.

I know what my friend is saying, but I'm 64 and I still don't look at myself as a *"growed up person"*. There are many who agree, but alas, for very different reasons. There are those who want to be perpetually young and are reluctant to acknowledge their age in public, or in private. It's not that they see old age as a punishment, but they look on youth as being constantly ready for the next adventure in living.

I'm still growing and I look forward to it. I've enjoyed life more in the last seven years than I ever have before. One reason for this is that I know that just around the corner there's an experience waiting for me. An experience I've never had before, and, unlike Sisyphus, I'll never experience it again. This same friend tells me I've wanted to be old since I was 14, and I guess she's right. I'll tell you this, I look forward to being 10,000 years old! It's like the last verse of the song, *Amazing Grace*, "When we've been there ten thousand years, Bright shinning as the sun, We've no less days to sing God's praise than when we'd first begun."

For some people, these are just the words of a song. They rhyme, sound good, and move the heart. For me they are all of that — and more. They move my heart and mind, they move me, they are gospel. For some these are *"church words."* They sound good in church, "but when you go out into the *real* world there's a difference," they say.

Father Rhor once used the expression that those of us who follow Christ are "people who live in the Church (the Body of Christ) and go to the world, not people who live in the world and go to Church." There's meaning there, and a wealth of reality.

Earlier this year I downloaded some pictures taken by the Hubbell Space Telescope of a star system being formed seven-thousand light years away. Now that's *reality*, and my God set those stars in motion. So when you hear me sing the words of the last verse of *Amazing Grace*, you can tell me that I'm off key, and I've no voice for singing, but don't tell me about your *real world*.

A long time ago Jesus told me about people who try to separate religion and faith, from the *real* world. *"No one can serve two masters. He will either hate one and love the other, or be devoted to one and despise the other. You cannot serve God and mammon.*[money, the real world]*"* (Luke 16:13)

When faith tells me something that just doesn't fit in your *real world*, I call to mind the words Leonard Bernstein wrote for his musical production, **Mass**. *"For the Word was at the birth of the beginning. It made the heavens and the earth and set them spinning, And for several million years It's withstood all our forums and fine ideas. It's been rough. It's been rough but it appears to be winning! There are people who doubt it and shout it out loud. There are local vocal yokels who we know collect a crowd. They can fashion a rebuttal that's as subtle as a sword, But they're never gonna scuttle the Word of the Lord."*

There's so very much more of God's creation to be discovered that space travel seems our natural destiny. And I'll never be able to say, "Finally I'm a growed up person."

31 — I TOUCH THE FUTURE - I TEACH

Generally, I prefer quotations to stand the test of time before I make them part of my ignition system. Two I heard recently, however, are exceptions.

The 28th of January was the tenth anniversary of the Challenger explosion which took the lives of all aboard. One of those was Christa McAuliffe, a school teacher. She is quoted as having said, *"I touch the future - I teach."*

The second quote came through retiring Senator Bill Bradley. During a television interview he recalled some advice Robert Kennedy gave him when he entered politics. Bradley had asked Kennedy what he should aim for as a senator, and Kennedy replied, *"Strive to be fully human."*

We're not all teachers and we're not all politicians, but all of us do teach, and all of us should be political. Many, of course will deny any identification with either, but especially with politics.

I looked up *"politic"* the other day. It comes from the Greek word *politikos*, which has to do with things pertaining to a citizen. The first definition is: *having practical wisdom; prudent; shrewd; diplomatic.* The second is: *crafty; unscrupulous.* As Shakespeare might have noted, it is unfortunately true, and truly unfortunate that in our day and time to be called a *politician* is to be branded with the second definition.

In a similar way we have emasculated the term *teach*. It comes from the Old English *taecan* which is a sign, or a symbol. Its first meaning is *to show, or help to learn.* Most teaching, like most learning, is not limited to a classroom. It has its beginning and consummation in a relationship.

Daily I am in contact with others, at least indirectly. Some of these contacts are deep and overflowing, some are simply superficial, but all are relationships of one sort or another. In all of them I can be a teacher, and in all of them I can touch the future. It is in this that I realize the truth of Fr. DeMello's observation that awareness is the very essence of spiritual growth.

It's a shame that so very often the second definition of politics — crafty and unscrupulous — is the one that is taken for granted. The remedy I try to use to defend myself against this comes, aptly enough, from the scripture. *"Stop judging, that you may not be judged. For as you judge, so will you be judged, and the measure with which you measure will be measured out to you."* (Mt. 7:1-2)

I can just hear people saying, *"That's all right for church, **but** in the real world..."* Some will say that my kind of talk is okay for the 'pink cloud set', but among real human beings, life is different. That's what I treasure about Kennedy's advice to Bill Bradley, *"Strive to be fully human."*

In the so-called 'real world' I find the limitations people put on human nature to be pathetic. I'm not blind to the character defects, the sins, the crimes, the horrors which individual human beings commit, and are capable of. Nor am I ignorant of the virtuous deeds, the acts of love and caring which individual human beings carry out, and are capable of. One does not balance the other, nor is one redeemed by the other.

What makes human nature and human beings so admirable is that God loved us, and redeemed us, and, in the

Incarnation, became one with us. If I must judge (and at times I seem incapable of not judging), then I should judge rightly. I should judge the acts, and not the person. For I can know, and see, and feel the acts of another. But I can never know, and see, and feel the essence, the very person, of another human being.

To be fully human is to **be in the process of knowing that I've been touched by God,** and that I live in the midst of people who have been touched by God.

I live in a world that cries out ever more loudly, and persistently, *"This is the real world. Get used to it."* However, Jesus tells me that although I am in that world, I must not be *of* that world. I am *of* the world that Jesus, in the Incarnation, has loved, and forgiven, and redeemed. I am brother to God, who became human, and showed me what it means to be *fully human.*

With Christa McAuliffe I have touched the future because in ways ordinary and small I am a teacher. With Bill Bradley I strive to be fully human because Jesus has shown me what that means.

32 — THE LESSON OF THE FORGOTTEN WALLET

Sometimes I'm amazed, sometimes I'm amused, at how the ordinary things of life help me to understand the scripture. I forgot my wallet the other day, and it was this ordinary little thing that helped me understand more clearly what Paul was talking about in part of his letter to the Romans.

Here's a passage from Paul's letter: *"Does it follow that the Law itself is sin? Of course not! What I mean is that I should not have known sin except for the law. I should not, for instance have known what it means to covet if the Law had not said, 'You shall not covet' But it was this commandment that sin took advantage of to produce all kinds of covetousness in me, for when there is no Law sin is dead. Once when there was no law I was alive; but when the commandment came, sin came to life and I died."* (Romans 7:7-9 from the Jerusalem Bible)

I remembered this passage when I forgot my wallet. It happened this way: I'd come to the *Common Sense* newspaper office last week to turn in my column. As I was leaving, I wanted to buy a candy bar that was on sale there to raise money for one purpose or another. I reached for my wallet — but I didn't have it. The lack of candy didn't worry me but I did become anxious about driving home without my driver's license. What if I had a wreck? The law says I'm supposed to have my license with me. I knew I could explain it to the police, yet never-the-less I was anxious and I drove home with extra care. It dawned on me that when I was driving to the paper's office I was not the least bit anxious. I thought I had my license with me, so I was unaware, and unconcerned with the law. When I was unaware of the Law I was quite alive and happy. That was then, this was now. When I became aware that I didn't have my driver's license with me, I became aware of the law. I was nervous, and upset, and not quite as "free" as I was when I drove in.

Of course, the parallel between what Paul was saying and my situation falls short, but it does help me understand what Paul was saying. He goes on to say, *"The Law is scared, and what it commands is sacred, just and good."* He then asks how can this good thing give him such problems. I could say the same thing about the law requiring me to carry my driver's license with me. It's good, and it has a good purpose, so how come I got so up tight when I forgot my wallet?

What Paul said is, *"The Law, as we all know is spiritual; but I am unspiritual."* Can you imagine **Saint** Paul saying that he is *un*spiritual. Well, of course, he's supposed to say that, he's a saint, but we know he's really spiritual. If he didn't say that he wouldn't be humble, and he wouldn't be a saint.

Wrong! Wrong! He says that because it's true, and if he doesn't speak the truth, he wouldn't be a saint. But he is a saint, so how could he be *"unspiritual"*? The answer to that question is not that he didn't become a saint until after he was dead. He was declared a saint after he was dead, **but** that is because of the way he lived before he was dead.

There are all sorts of things the Church requires before declaring a person a saint and one of them is that you have to be dead. There are a number of miracles that are also required. As far as I'm concerned, there are four other basic requirements to be a saint, declared or otherwise. 1) I gotta know that I'm unspiritual. 2) I gotta want to be spiritual. 3) I gotta accept the fact that going from one to the other is a process. 4) I gotta realize that I'm not in charge of the process, but I am willing to be part of it.

Paul fits all four of those requirements. Listen to what this holy man says, and see if you can relate. I know I can, *"... though the will to do what is good is in me, the performance is not. .... In fact, this seems to be the rule, that every single time I want to do good it is something evil that comes to hand. Who will rescue me...?"* (Romans 7:18-25) Then, as Fr. Rohr notes, Paul seems to jump with joy as he shouts that salvation is through and from Jesus Christ.

I'm glad I forgot my wallet last week, it gave me a chance to remember that God has a will and a way to work in my life. The effectiveness of His work depends on my willingness, my cooperation — not on how good I am.

I'm not a parent, so let me ask those of you who are, *"Do you love your children because they are good? Or are they good because you love them?"* Fr. Rohr asks the same question about our relationship with God. *"Does God love us because we are good? Or are we good because God loves us?"*

The love of God changes me. That change is a process, and I'm willing to be part of it. Sometimes I get impatient with the pace of it, and try to get holy by doing it my way. Yes sir, I'm glad I forgot my wallet, it helped me put a whole lot of things in focus.

33 — FREEDOM IS IN THE LITTLE THINGS

In my spiritual growth I encounter a couple of stumbling blocks all too frequently. One of them is the excuse I use for not dealing with any number of *minor* faults. The other is my art of making any fault into a minor fault. After thirty years of pastoring, I realize that this does not entitle me to membership in a minority group.

You may recognize this stumbling block: *"Well it* (choose any minor fault you wish here: impatience, bad language, little white lies, etc.) *is not all that important. Besides, I've got some really big faults to deal with."* I might fool many people with an excuse like that, but I know the truth. I'm seeking to enjoy the freedom that comes from not having to deal with the problem. Freedom!! Well, now that's quite an attraction. After all, didn't God create us to be free?

That's a good line, but to accept as God's freedom the ease that comes from not dealing with problems, large or small, is like accepting the head on a beer as the real thing. It tickles the nose, but it ain't beer.

A few times I've had a taste of the real thing, of real freedom, and from then on it has been impossible to settle for second best without really knowing it. I can look at the leisure I get by not dealing with a problem, and can call it freedom, but to paraphrase an old Texas politician, *"I've known real freedom. I've worked with it. I've enjoyed it, and the leisure of avoidance is not real freedom."*

St. Paul, and others, say that sin is slavery. That doesn't mean that license is freedom. The first meaning of license is the formal permission to do something. But I must bear in mind the warning of Chesterton (I think), *"Just because I have a right to do a thing, doesn't mean it's the right thing to do."*

Freedom, to me, is being able to avoid what I know I should avoid, and being able to do what I know I should do. Anyone who has ever tried to quit smoking, or drinking, or eating chocolate knows what I'm talking about. Of course if you can't relate to those, or similar addictions, perhaps you can relate to a difficulty I've had in breaking a tendency to judge others as wimps because they have those addictions.

A while back I wrote a column about making mountains out of molehills. I borrowed a much used phrase and called it, *Pole Vaulting Over Mouse Droppings*. This is the very opposite of the stumbling block I have in mind today. I've developed an art form that enables me to understand just about anything I do as something that's not really important in the grand scheme of things, and that doesn't really bother anyone.

If I need to, I can always fall back on this excuse, *"Hey who's gonna be hurt if I put off dealing with these little faults? The people will still have daily Mass, I'll still visit the sick, write my column, console the sorrowing, hear confessions, and administer the other sacraments. So who's gonna be hurt?"*

This reminds me of that story in Jeremiah about those guys who were plotting against him. *"The men of Judah and the citizens of Jerusalem said, 'Let us contrive a plot against Jeremiah. It will not mean the loss of instruction from the priests, nor of counsel from the wise, nor of messages from the prophets. And so, let us destroy him by his own tongue; let us carefully note his every word.'"* (Jeremiah 18:18)

Who's gonna suffer if I lose my temper? I rarely get mad in public. But asking who will suffer is a distracting if not phony question. I ask it to keep me from asking the real question, and dealing with the real problem. The real question is: Who's gonna be hurt if I refuse to grow spiritually?

The answer to the question, of course, is me. I'm the first person to be hurt. Next come the number of people I'll interact with in my daily life. I'm not talking about the big deal, the *really* important things. I'm talking about the ordinary things in my life.

Never underestimate the power of the ordinary. Every now and then we see on TV a building being imploded, that is, purposely destroyed. It's an amazing scene, it's an extraordinary event, and it's fascinating to watch. But the ordinary little termite does just as much damage. Not as quickly, but a whole lot more often. Ordinary things can lead to profound things. The movie that impresses so many people each year at Christmas time, *It's a Wonderful Life,* is based on the ordinary events in one person's life.

When the runner wins the race and crosses the finish line, we all cheer, but what made it possible was the ordinary act of repeatedly putting one foot in front of the other. For all of us ordinary people, I'll share with you a extraordinary truth I'm discovering, "It's the ordinary things in life that make the extraordinary things possible."

34 — CLIMBING DOWN THE MOUNTAINS

I came across a rather unusual quote in Father Rohr's book *"Simplicity."* He had been writing about the need to let go of the many things in life that have always been considered necessities. The quote was from the eminent psychiatrist, Carl Jung.

In his old age Jung described his pilgrimage through life in this way: *"My journey consisted in climbing down ten thousand ladders so that now at the end of my life I can extend the hand of friendship to this little clod of earth that I am."*

Richard commented that Jung was indeed a free man, having let go of so many false securities. My comment is: If that be true, then how many ladders must *I* climb down? I prefer to use the image of climbing down mountains, rather than ladders, but the point is the same.

One of the most obvious images for some people is the pedestal from which some priests reign. I used to say, *"The people put the priest on a pedestal."* This may well be true, but I can not remain on anyone's pedestal unless I'm willing to do so. A major problem with letting the people put me up on a pedestal is that there will come a time when, instead of putting me up on a pedestal, they will simply be putting up with me.

The Letter to the Hebrews makes it clear that the priest is chosen from among the people, not because he is different from, but because he is the same as. *"Every high priest is taken from among men and made their representative before God, to offer gifts and sacrifices for sins. He is able to deal patiently with the ignorant and erring,* **for he himself is beset by weakness and so,** *for this reason, must make sin offerings for himself as well as for the people."* (Hebrews 5:1-3) That's a mighty high mountain to climb down from, and yet I was never really up there. It was all an illusion.

There was a time when I thought that the real mountain to climb was the one called "Power." It seemed that everybody who was anybody had power. If you had no power you were a nobody. But then along came a guy named Paul who claimed he was a nobody. And almost two thousand years after he died he still wields influence among millions of people. That's power!! And it is he who quoted the Lord as saying, *"My grace is sufficient for you, for power is made perfect in weakness."*

And how can I forget what Jesus said to Pilate when Pilate claimed to have the power of life and death over Him: *"You would have no power over me were it not given you from above."* (John 19:11) So power, real power, is a gift, a grace, not a mountain to be climbed. Again, a mountain to climb **down from** that I never actually climbed up.

Having authority — that's a worthy mountain. I can't remember the first time I had authority over anything, but it was probably at home or in grade school. If the experience I had in the Air Force is any gauge, I more than likely made a mess of it. I was given authority over some clean-up detail in the Air Force once. I did a much better job of showing my authority than I did of getting the area cleaned up. If I had just paid attention to American History in high school I'd have known, as Jefferson did, that he who governs least, governs best. Of course Jesus told me how I should have acted, *"The kings of the Gentiles lord it over them.... but among you it shall not be so. Let the greatest be as the least and the leader as the servant."* (Luke 22:25-27) Authority is a mountain I climbed, or thought I did, but I have to climb down.

Sean, a friend of mine, told me something very important about mountain tops. On the top of the mountain the view is great, but it is often above the tree line where little or nothing lives or grows. It's in the green valley, at the bottom of the mountain, where there's real growth and life.

I've told you of three mountains that I often climbed incorrectly: the Pedestal; Power; and Authority, but there are many more, such as money, manipulation, etc. But within each of these three, I have had ten thousand opportunities to climb down.

Climbing down a mountain or a ladder is not abandoning a goal. It's not giving up. It's surrendering to reality. It's owning my weakness and embracing my real strength. You remember the difference between giving up and surrendering, don't you? To give up, to quit, is to say, "I can't do this!" To surrender is to invite God into my life through my neighbor, or the Spirit by saying, "I can't do this *alone!*"

I hate to quit. I hate to give up, but I'm beginning to love surrender. For me, this often means I have to climb down mountains I once thought were worth climbing up.

35 — IS THE HOLY SPIRIT A PARAKEET?

Getting ready for the Sixth Sunday of Easter reminded me of a question a youngster posed a few years ago. The child asked, *"Is the Holy Spirit a Parakeet, or a Dove?"*

I had no difficulty understanding his problem because I had the same problem as a child. When the Gospel was read, the child heard the priest say that Jesus was going to send another Parakeet to be with the apostles. Of course the word was *Paraclete,* and I think the confusion is natural because what we have done is simply take a Greek word and placed it in the English text without bothering to translate it.

I have been trying to learn Spanish so I can celebrate Mass with Spanish speaking people and I wondered how the Spanish handled the confusion. They did it right. They translated the word. In the Spanish text, Jesus promises to send a *Defensor*. In English we might translate Paraclete to something like Defense Attorney.

The Book of Revelation tells me that the devil accuses God's people day and night. (Rev.12:10) To be my Defense Attorney in the face of the accusations of the devil is the one of the many purposes of the Holy Spirit.

In our society, defense attorneys sometimes get a bad rap. Their duty is to use every legal technicality in the book to defend their clients, and the result, according to some, is that frequently the guilty go free.

It may sound great to have the Holy Spirit as my Defense Advocate, but if I signed up the Holy Spirit as my *Defensor*, my

Attorney with any hope of being acquitted, I'd be in for a surprise. Because according to the promise of Jesus, The Paraclete is the Spirit of Truth. So if I've done what the devil accuses me of, the Spirit's not gonna to try to get me off. Being the Spirit of Truth, He is going to use every trick in the book to get me to plead guilty. What kind of Defense Advocate is that?

Consider this: If a lawyer is defending a client who's actually guilty, and who is convicted, the lawyer lost the case. However, if the *Paraclete*, the *Defensor* is defending me against the accusations of the devil, and I'm actually guilty, the Paraclete, the Defensor in my case has won only *if* I plead guilty.

Remember what old Simeon said when Jesus was presented in the Temple? *"This child is destined for the rise and fall of many in Israel, and to be a sign of contradiction."* Talk about a contradiction. I'd expect a victory to be declared if I was found innocent, not if I had to plead guilty. So I ask you, "What kind of help is the Holy Spirit to me?"

What would you say to a lawyer who told you, "I expect you to be found guilty, but that's the good news." I know what I'd say. I'd say, "You're fired."

I share in a Penitential Rite in every Mass I celebrate. Unless this is just an empty ritual, I'm actually accusing myself of sin. I'm pleading guilty. If I'm not just mindlessly mouthing words, if I'm really serious about this, then I'm working with my Defensor, the Paraclete, the Holy Spirit.

I think this is what's happening: the Spirit of God, the Spirit of Truth, is working to help me accept and face reality without fear. I can picture a courtroom with me as the defendant, the devil as the prosecuting attorney, and the Holy Spirit as my lawyer. My lawyer keeps telling me to plead guilty while the prosecutor keeps yelling, *"You're guilty, you're guilty and you're going to jail for years!!"* But my lawyer keeps patting me on the shoulder and saying, *"Don't worry! Fear not!"* Brother, that takes faith.

Isaiah, who lived hundreds of years before the Lord Jesus, gives me reason for faith, reason to fear not. He writes of the Suffering Servant of the Lord, and scripture scholars everywhere say this refers to the Messiah. *"He was pierced for our offenses, crushed for our sins. Upon him was the chastisement that makes us whole, by his stripes we were healed. We had all gone astray like sheep, each following his own way; But the Lord laid upon him the guilt of us all."*

John tells me, *"If we say 'We are without sin' we deceive ourselves and the truth is not in us."* (I Jn 1:8) So if I want the Lord to take my guilt I have to acknowledge it. That's why my defense counsel, the Paraclete, the Defensor, keeps urging me to plead guilty. Don't you see? I can't say that the Lord has taken my guilt unless I claim it as mine — I have to plead guilty.

The Lord gave me a defense counsel, a Paraclete, a Defensor, and his job is not to get me off, but to help me plead guilty. Now ain't that strange.

36 — WHAT IN THE WORLD IS GRACE?

First I want you to know that I am **NOT** a Theologian. I'm a human being, a Christian, a priest, and a pastor — in that order. I'm not exactly sure what a Theologian is, but I know I'm not one of them. When I was asked by the Editor of *Common Sense* to write a column explaining just what Grace is, I was more than a little hesitant. However, I was assured that she was not looking for a theological document, so I agreed to do it.

To put it simply, and I have to put it simply because that's the only way I can even begin to talk about Grace, my answer to the question: *"What in the world is Grace?"* is: **God in the world is Grace**.

Over thirty years ago I had a course in Grace in the seminary. The Prof. told us at the beginning of the course, in nine words, just what Grace is: *"Grace is nothing other than the life of God."* At the end of the course he gave a test which included an essay question, *"In one hundred words, or less, explain what Grace is."* I choose to answer in those nine words, and I got full credit.

From the Baltimore Catechism I learned about Actual Grace and Sanctifying Grace. Some people speak of Transitory Grace, and Permanent Grace. If you're looking for anything like that here, forget it. I talk about Grace in three ways, Grace is the life of God; it's a Gift; and it's a relationship.

The beginning of the Bible tells me, in story form, how the human race fell out of a loving relationship with God. The whole of the rest of the Bible tells about God's promise to restore the relationship, how He did it, and how He continues to do it.

The late Fr. Anthony DeMello, S.J. told a story of the *Little Fish* and I recounted it in the initial chapter of this book. It's a profoundly simple story that directly relates to the topic of Grace, so I'll share it again: An older and wiser fish observed a little fish frantically swimming back and forth in a pond, and asked what he was doing. The small fish replied, "I was told that a fish needs water to live. I'm looking for the water." The older fish, remembering his younger days, didn't laugh. He simply said, "Little fish, the water is all around you. You're in the water." The little one looked up and down, and all around, swallowed, sniffed a bit, and unconvinced, he said, "It can't be that simple!" And with a swish of his tail, he swam off to look for the water. The older fish didn't laugh, or smile. Remembering his younger days, he was filled with hope.

I think Leonard Bernstein says it best in a song from "Mass": *"Sing God a simple song. Make it up as you go along. God loves all simple things, for God is the simplest of all."*

Grace is not something I can measure in pounds, or gallons, or feet or yards. When I think of Grace I think more in terms of quality than of quantity. Grace is not something that matures, or wears out. Grace doesn't change, but it changes me — if I let it. Grace is not something I can earn, or be worthy of. This is why Fr. Rohr says, *"Worthiness is not the issue."* If I want to grow in Grace, two things, and a third, are needed: Awareness, Acceptance, and Willingness.

Grace is the Life of God. Where is God? God is everywhere. What is God? God is Reality. He tells us, *"I am who I am."* That's reality, of course, a spiritual reality. I used to limit reality to what I could sense with my five senses. This implied that my thoughts, my dreams, my feelings had no reality. God is real, and so is Grace, but He is not limited, nor defined by physical reality.

Grace is a Gift. Funny thing about a Gift is that, it is not simply something that's given, it must also be **received**. Years ago I proposed marriage to a young lady. I offered her a ring. She said "no" to the proposal, so the ring never became a gift. God continually offers to share His life with me through the sacraments, through a living faith, and though love of neighbor. The offer is always there, but unless I accept it, it never becomes Grace for me.

Grace is a relationship. Paul often uses marriage as an example when he speaks of the relation of Christ and the Church — God and His people. The more I am aware of God's willingness to be in relationship with me the more I know what Grace is. Fr. DeMello wrote a book in which he says that the one essential item in spiritual growth is *awareness*. When asked to amply the idea, he said, "*Awareness, awareness, awareness.*" The name of the book, by the way, is "*Awareness*".

John Bannister Tabb, the poet, made theologians envious in his three line poem about God, about Grace:

> I see Thee in the distant blue
> but in the violets dell of dew,
> I see and taste Thee too.

37 — "WHY" IS MORE IMPORTANT THAN "WHEN"

We celebrated the birthday of John, the Baptizer last week. I've been a priest for over thirty years, and last week I discovered something about this feast I had never thought of. I figured you might be interested.

I have to start with Christmas. Long ago I learned how the Church selected the date for this feast. I'm told that, except for royalty and wealthy people, accurate records of births and deaths were not of great importance, especially the births of the poor — and perhaps, most importantly, the records of poor people born in a stable. I'm also told that for the first two or three hundred years of Christianity the only major feast of the Lord that was celebrated was the Resurrection.

There came a time when people wanted to celebrate the birthday of the Lord. An effort was made to pin-point the historical event, but a more earnest effort was made to spotlight theological truths. Naturally the reason the stress was on theological truths was that the early Church had to contend with the paganism of its day. A great pagan festival, in late December, celebrated the return of the sun god. This is the winter solstice from which point in time the days begin to get longer.

The Church, remembering that Jesus had proclaimed that He is the Light of the world and the Son of God, deemed December 25th an appropriate date to celebrate His birth. Once that date became fixed, it was a simple matter of counting back nine months to celebrate the feast we know as the Annunciation. It marks the time when the Angel Gabriel came to Mary with the first Good News. This is when Mary, through the power of the Holy Spirit, conceived the Child Jesus.

The Angel Gabriel gave Mary some more amazing news, *"Know this too: your kinswoman Elizabeth has, in her old age, herself conceived a son, and she whom people called barren is now in her sixth month, for nothing is impossible to God."* (Luke 1:36-37) This gives us a date for the birth of John, the Baptizer. In March Elizabeth was in her sixth month, so we celebrate John's birth in June.

None of these dates are rooted in historical accuracy, but all of them are founded in theological reality. We celebrate the birth of Jesus, the Light of the World, the Son of God, in late December, around the winter solstice when the days begin to get longer. In June, near the summer solstice, we celebrate the birth of John, the Baptizer. After the summer solstice the days begin to get shorter. John said of himself, *"He (Christ) must increase, I must decrease."*

I never gave much thought to those nine months that Mary was pregnant. This may be, not only because I'm a man, but because I'm a celibate man. I never thought of her pregnancy as source of spiritual nourishment for me. But that feast of the Birth of John, the Baptizer, got me to thinking.

Mary got pregnant because she was totally open to the working of the Holy Spirit within her. When she learned that her senior citizen cousin was not only pregnant, but very pregnant, she did the normal thing and went to help. When I think about Mary going out to help I think, "How like Mother Teresa she was." Then I remember that Mary came first. The point that is made in my mind is, "How very human Mary was."

Some spiritual guru of mine told me somewhere along the line, "The Son of God didn't become human because he was tired of being Divine. He became human to show me how very much His Father wanted me to be part of His family." My spiritual guide also told me that being tired of being human is not the way to become part of the Divine family.

This is one of the things that I see in Mary's pregnancy — it's such a very human thing. I'm quite sure that the Divinity of her Child did not exempt her from morning sickness, and other unpleasantries of pregnancy.

In a spiritual, but none-the-less real way, when I was Baptized, Mary's Child began a living relationship with me. That relationship comes to full stature in me, not because I grow tired of being human, but because I become comfortable with being human. Because I become comfortable doing the ordinary human things of life in a growing union with the Divine.

When Mary's pregnancy came to full term, she did not cease to be human. When my spiritual growth, dare I say, my spiritual pregnancy, comes to full term — that is, when I die — I'll not cease to be human. I'll just become totally comfortable being human, and in union with my Divine Father. All these thoughts came to me with the celebration of the Feast of the Birth of John the Baptizer, and how its date is dependent on Mary's pregnancy.

38 — BUTTERFLIES IN MY HEART

Fathers Martell, McCaver, and I are in Miami to study Spanish. It's the middle of July, and wouldn't you know it, the air conditioning is broken, but all goes well — we're learning a little Spanish.

With the weekend free, I went to see my cousin, Dorothy Ann, and we took in a place called Butterfly World. They have every kind of Butterfly I ever heard of — and many more. Of course, they also have the flora on which they feed. Did you know that butterflies make a feast of bananas, and the average life span of many butterflies is just a few days?

These were not just dead butterflies pinned and under glass. They are alive, and flying all over. We walked among them, and, at times, the butterflies would light on my hat and shoulder. The people and butterflies are in the same screened in room. "Room" is the wrong word to use. It's actually a screened in area in which there are trees, flowers, and streams. The butterflies and people play together. There are also frequent and clear warnings that handling or stealing even dead butterflies is strictly forbidden.

In a separate screened in area there are humming birds, finches, and all the plants they need to sustain life. Never have I seen such colorful birds. I mean I have several hummers and many finches that come to my garden at different times of the year, but I've never seen anything like the number and variety as they have at Butterfly World.

I recalled the words of the Gospel when Jesus was talking about how beautifully God had clothed the birds of the air and the flowers of the field, and how much more we meant to God than birds and flowers.

The metamorphose of the lowly caterpillar to the magnificent butterfly brought to mind the words Paul quoted to the Corinthians about the eye not having seen, the ear not having heard, nor had it entered into the mind of man the wonderful things that God has prepared for those who love him.

The caterpillar is not all that endearing to look at, and it's not the favorite of gardeners. But just look at what it becomes. Of course, it has to die. Again I think of the words of Jesus about the grain of wheat that remains just a grain of wheat unless it dies. But when it dies — Wow!! I heard recently about some seeds that had been discovered in a tomb in China. They had lain dormant for over a thousand years, but when they were planted, they grew.

The caterpillar, without knowing what it will become, prepares to die. Guided by instinct it wraps itself in a cocoon. Without knowing why it places itself in a state of life that will inevitably lead to a change that, even for us thinking beings, is difficult to imagine or understand.

I don't know the why — or the how — of what I will become after my death. But I accept, as the word of God, that my eye has not seen, my ear has not heard, nor has it entered into my mind the wonderful life that God has prepared for those who love him.

I am guided by more than instinct. I know that I am going to die. Instinct doesn't tell me how to prepare for a dying that will lead to something far, far better than the short, but beautiful life of the butterfly. I have the saints. I have the Scripture. I have the testimony of God Himself.

The saints, the scripture, and God Himself present me with something far more than a list of, *Thou shalt* and *Thou shalt not*. I can look at the last judgment scene in the Gospel (Mt. 25: 31-45) and see that as the caterpillar wraps itself in the lowly ordinary things of the earth to prepare for death, so I should wrap myself in deeds of sharing and caring with the common everyday ordinary people of this earth.

A few years ago David Peterson brought to my attention a bit of scripture that tells me so very clearly what I can, and should, do to prepare for a metamorphose far beyond anything I've ever dreamed of. *"You have been told what is good and what the Lord requires of you: Only to do the right and to love goodness, and to walk humbly with your God."* (Micah 6:8)

The next time I see butterflies in my garden I'll recall what great things God has done for the little caterpillar, and I just know He'll do something even better for me. Air conditioning may, or may not, be part of it.

39 — EMILY WAS A GOOD OLE GAL

Let me tell you about Emily. She's dead, you know. Been dead for some time now. She was a good ole gal, and the impression she made lingers with me to this day. I met Emily while I was pastor at Nativity. She was a resident of a nursing home. I thought she was a bit young to be in a nursing home. The truth is that she was young, as far as nursing home residents go. It wasn't her age that got her there, it was her health.

I used to visit the nursing home on Friday mornings. I remember the day I met Emily. That was the day they started using a strawberry air freshener to overcome the usual fragrance of nursing homes. I recall because my allergy to it made my throat fuzzy. I had given Communion to one of my regulars, and we were just talking, when we were disturbed by an unusual noise that sounded like pots and pans knocking against each other. It seemed to be right outside the door, then without any other preamble the door opened, and in stepped Emily.

She was using a walker to which was loosely attached a metal ash tray, a metal drinking cup, and several other things of undetermined purpose. The walker had wheels on it, but they didn't work well, and so the whole contraption sort of bounced along.

Emily was a frail lady, and because she was so thin, she appeared much taller than she was. She stood in the doorway, looked at me over the top of her glasses and said, *"You must be the priest they told me about. I'm Emily, but everybody calls me 'Ole Hop-a-long' cause of this damned walker that doesn't work right. I'd* be hard pressed to sneak up on anybody. I guess you brought Communion. Hope you brought enough to include me."

That was the beginning of a relationship that grew to include many people in the parish. Emily was not outspoken, but she was plain spoken. I remember one time we were talking about Grace. I told her that Grace was a gift from God, it's free. She replied, *"Sure it is, but don't you forget, 'There's no such thing as a free lunch..'"* As her life drew to a close she explained to me exactly what she meant.

One time when I came to see her she was in bed. *"I'm really down today, Father, tell me a joke,"* she pleaded. Then she cleared a place on her bed and invited me to sit down. I hesitated thinking of the rule about sitting on a patient's bed. She noticed, laughed aloud, and bounced about saying, *"It'd really be funny if the nurse came in and caught us in bed together."* Another time she begged me to stay just a while longer while she smoked a cigarette. With anger she complained, *"I can't even smoke a butt without somebody watching. They're so afraid I'll burn the damn place down."*

People in the parish got to know her. They made sure she was invited to the Christmas decorating party, and a Spring luncheon. But the time came when she couldn't get out and around. She enjoyed a cold beer every now and then, but the time came when this too was denied her.

As one thing after another was denied her, she would respond in anger. She'd blame God now and then, but as often as she did she'd tell me, *"I don't understand God. I'm not really mad at Him, and I don't really blame Him, but I sure don't understand Him."*

One day she looked at me with tears in her eyes and asked, *"Why do these people talk to me like I'm a child? I know I can't have this or that, or do this or that, but they don't have to treat me like a child. Do they?"* I wondered then how often I had spoken in just that way to grown-up people just because they were sick in mind or body, and I promised myself I'd never do it again.

The circulation in one of her legs became a problem and she told me that they were going to have to cut it off. She looked at me and laughed a bit and said, *"Now what on earth does God want with my leg? He's got everything else. What does he want with my leg?"*

The operation was a success, but the patient died. Oh, she didn't die right away, but she did die. She told me after the operation, *"I didn't need that leg anyway, Hell, I never learned to dance."* Sometimes I was surprised at the language Emily used. I'm sure she talked to God the same way, and I'm sure God loved her.

Shortly before she died she told me, *"You know Father, you said that Grace is a gift an I said there's no such thing a free lunch. Well, I was right. I had to let go of just about everything to get hold of this free gift. It's been tough too. I'm not complaining. I just wanted you to know. But I didn't have nothing when I came into this world an it looks like I'll not have much when I go out."* Emily had a lot when she died, and she left a lot behind — it's called wisdom.

40 — AS LONG AS WE REMEMBER ... HUH??

In the last year with the death of so many of our priests and many other people whom I love, I've had ample opportunity to think about death. One of the things that I've heard fairly often at funerals is, *"As long as we remember her/him, he/she is not really dead."* Or words to that effect.

Well, as the late President, Richard Nixon, often said, *"I want to make one thing perfectly clear."* If my continued life after death should fall victim to dependence on the fragile memory of human kind, I'd be in one heck of a shape. It is, indeed, a hope of mine that I live my life in such a way that should a person from time to time remember me, that person would be the better for it.

But that's not what will keep me alive. My mother has been dead for over fifty years now. My father for thirty years. I remember them both — from time to time. I remember the lessons they tried to teach, and I think I am the better for it. But they live now, and enjoy life, even during those long stretches of time when the duties of my state in life prevent me from consciously averting to their continuing life.

So when I recall the dead, it is not to keep them alive, it's to make my life more meaningful than it would be without the recall.

What an awesome responsibility it would be — giving another person life by keeping them in mind. Only God can fulfill that kind of responsibility and only God should have the credit.

There's another saying that I hear around funerals, *"Life goes on."* This is usually said indicating the responsibility to get on with the business of living life — in the here and the now — not in the past, or the hereafter. There is purpose here, and reality. The saying hardly ever refers to the life of the deceased as continuing.

A friend of mine, Don, used to use that saying frequently. With him it was one of the answers to all the disappointments and disasters in his life. The first time I remember him using it was after he had waited two weeks for his wife to join him in Memphis from up north, and then he was notified that she had run off with another man. I expected the worst from him, yet after a night of confronting the reality he greeted me the next morning with a smile and, *"Life goes on."*

When he died some years later, Wally and I and several friends buried him. His words came back to me. I could hear him saying, *"Life goes on."* I knew they were meant not only for me but for him. His life goes on. The prolonging of his life has nothing to do with my memory, but the enrichment of my life is somehow entwined with the way he lived his, and my memory of it.

But my life goes on, and I can enjoy it so much more because I remember, in the face of disasters and disappointments, that life, indeed, does go on, both here and hereafter.

Meeting disasters and disappointments, with a phrase like, *"Life goes on,"* is sometimes akin to getting used to a new pair of shoes. It's a little painful at first, and for a while I'm not sure I want to keep them. Then, after a while I get used them, I wonder how I ever got along without them. *Life goes on.*

I've got a few talents that I've really developed. One of them is worrying. People tell me, *"Don't worry."* I've never figured that out. Here's the one thing that I'm really good at — and people tell me not to do it! Another thing I do well is making mountains out of mole hills, disasters out of day time. Then Don comes along and tells me, "*Hey, it's no big deal, life goes on.*"

Don't you just hate it when they're right and you're wrong? I do.

"*Life goes on,*" aims at putting things in a perspective of reality. It aims at setting priorities in a framework of reality. What, after all, is really important here — the mountain I just worked so hard making, or the mole hill out of which I made it? The mole hill is important because it's real. The mountain is not important because it's not really real.

Father Richard Rohr says that God is the *Really Real*. So no matter what I make of a mole hill, it's only important if it's reality. And the only reason reality is important is because it's the only place God is.

Life goes on — both here and here after.

41 — COLLEGE KIDS KILL THEIR BABY!!

COLLEGE KIDS KILL THEIR BABY!!! What a horrible, horrible, horrible headline — and yet it's true. It halts the mind, freezes the heart — and yet it's true.

Not too long ago an Air Force Academy Cadet and his girl friend were arrested and charged with the murder of another young lady. It strains credulity — and yet it's true.

Just a few years back, in England, two ten year old boys kidnapped and killed a four year old, and in West Memphis, four children are sadistically killed by young people who, themselves, had left childhood not long ago.

Systems of Justice will certainly investigate, find fault, and assign a punishment. But is the primary purpose of investigation to find fault, and to assign punishment? I think not. The primary purpose of investigation is to discover hope.

I don't know the cause, or causes, for these and so many other totally outrageous actions. But I do know this: More and more people are over reacting to mundane situations, from traffic to television, in totally abominable ways.

The more I look at this vast and very complicated morass of human relationships, the more I wonder if the solution is not a great deal more simple than it would appear. For some reason or another, for most of us seriousness seems to rule out simplicity. Can't you just see Jesus coming to the table of world leaders working on the problems of world peace, or hunger, or poverty, and saying, *"I've found a solution for you — little children love one another."*

You and I know what the response would be. *"Who let Him in here? Thanks a lot Jesus, but we've got serious work to do. Why don't you get your people to fax our people, and we'll take a look at it. Keep in touch."*

Jesus was about redeeming the world — no small task. Seems odd He should start with the Jews. According to the scripture, they claimed to be among the world's most insignificant people.

Of course, Matthew, Mark, Luke, and John tell us that from time to time Jesus did preach to the multitudes. Very often, however, the multitude was totally out of the picture. Like the time John tells us that He fed over 5,000 people with just a few loaves and fishes. Then just a few verses later these same people are demanding a sign. Mark tells us that He went to some lengths to avoid the acclaim of the crowd.

My ministry as a priest is to preach the Good News; to offer the sacrifice of the Mass; to make the sacraments available to all; and to make the Bishop's care and concern felt among his people. This is a fairly simple description of what I'm supposed to be about, but sometimes I make a mess of it by complicating the simple. I mean, where's the glory in being successful in something that's so simple?

Jesus was about redeeming the world, and as His priest, that's what I am about. Strategic Plans and Missions are good and necessary. In fact I've invited Fr. Al Kirk to speak to the people of St. Joseph on just that subject.

I don't have any idea what to do about those kids who killed their baby, or those ten year olds who kidnapped and killed a four year old boy, or about the teenage killers from West Memphis. I don't know what to do about so very many other very serious tragedies throughout our world.

I do know this: what seems to work best for me is a simple sharing with others about how Jesus is acting in my life. I spend a lot of time writing this column, but I try to keep it simple. I spend a lot of time on my sermons — I write almost all of them — but I try to keep them simple. I go to the Federal Prison on Sunday nights — I gotta keep it simple. It's all in Spanish and my vocabulary is limited. I hear confessions at Search and I think those young people do more for my spiritual growth than I do for theirs.

One of the things I like about Search, Cursillo, Marriage Encounter, and Engaged Encounter is the simplicity of the approach in them. They are about personal spiritual growth. They are about the responsibility of sharing, not imposing, that personal spiritual growth. They are very simple in their ministry and their approach to it, but they wouldn't exist at all unless there had been some long range planning by somebody. I'm not very good at that sort of thing, but thank God other people are. Whether you are involved in complicated things — or in simple things — keep in mind these words of wisdom, *"Never let what you can't do get in the way of what you can do."*

42 — BOUGHT AND PAID FOR

Have you ever seen or heard something for a thousand times, and then all of a sudden you see in it or hear in it something you've never seen or heard before? It happens to me more often than I'd like to admit. When it happens to me I want to rush out and tell everyone about it. But when I do, I often get the reply, *"I knew that."* Then I begin to wonder how I could've missed that for all these years. Well, it happened again, and at the risk of seeming like the last person in the universe to get the joke, to understand the situation, I'll share it with you.

In January we observed the anniversary of the Supreme Court decision on abortion. On the 19th of January, which the Church reckons as the Second Sunday in Ordinary time, we had a reading from Paul's first letter to the Corinthians. (I Cor. 6:13-15 and 17-20)

In that section, Paul is laying it on the line for men who go to prostitutes. I've always found it interesting that Paul does not appeal to the government to make prostitution against the law on the grounds that it's harmful to the family, and therefore, harmful to society. He simply tells the men that, when they go to a prostitute, they become one with the prostitute. He points out that this is a contradiction in terms for men who claim to be one with Christ.

Paul says that the reason that it's a contradiction is, *"...that your body is a temple of the Holy Spirit ..., and that you are not your own for you have been purchased at a price."*

"You are not your own. You have been purchased..." I've heard people who have serious problems with alcohol and other drugs say, *"I'm not hurting anyone but me. It's my business, so butt out."* I've used it myself. I'm told that people with eating disorders, people in trouble with credit cards, and so on use this same justification.

On the Second Sunday in Ordinary Time, when I heard that letter from Paul being read, it occurred to me that people who think the government should make no laws against abortion also use the words, *"It's my body, it's my business."*

As a citizen of this great country, I do think that the government should be wary of making laws that restrict personal freedom. However, as a priest of Jesus Christ, and a proclaimer of God's Word, I am very aware of my responsibility to alert my fellow believers that we are not our own. That my body is not my own. That my very self has been purchased by the Blood of Christ Jesus. That I am duty bound, as a believer in Christ Jesus to glorify God in my body.

As a citizen of this country I enjoy the right to an immense amount of personal freedom guaranteed by law as long as I do no harm to the rights of my fellow citizens. Some will argue that the abuse of alcohol and other drugs and the acting out of other addictions *does* harm my fellow citizens. Some will say this is especially true in abortion. I have no argument with any of these assertions. But those arguments have nothing to do with what concerns me.

What concerns me is how I deal with bodily temptations. Paul tells me that I should not join my body to a prostitute, not because there's a civil law against it, but because I am already joined to Christ, and that joining has been paid for at a great price.

Every now and then I think I would really enjoy a drink — an alcoholic beverage. There's no law that says that I can't.

However, in my case, having just one drink would be a serious abuse of my body and I cannot justify it by saying, "*It's my body. It's my business.*" I can't do that because I — body, soul, and spirit — have been purchased. No governmental law, or the lack of it, can ever change that.

I have no argument with non-believers about the laws of our country, or the lack of them. The laws of my country — and how I respect them — surely define my standing as citizen of this country. But that's not the criterion that defines my standing with my fellow believers and my standing before my God. That's defined by how I respect the Word of God.

I may certainly fall short and miss the mark now and then. But reconciliation with my God is not attained by denying guilt with the statement: *"It's my body. It's my business."* Reconciliation is regained by acknowledging guilt and realizing that I am not my own — that I have been purchased at a great price. Some may say this is just imposing a guilt trip — or a guilt complex. That may be because they are not aware of the difference between a guilt *complex* and a guilty *conscience*. A guilt complex prevents one from living fully in society. A guilty conscience calls one to repentance and the fullness of life.

43 — SURRENDERING ISN'T QUITTING!!

Ken DeWitt died in the morning. Around nine o'clock it was. I remember thinking, *"How unlike Ken to die so early so in the morning, just as the day's getting started with so many things to plan."* Estell Coleman gave him Communion just minutes before he died, but that was an accident of timing, not a plan.

I've known Ken since the time I was an associate at St. Ann in Bartlett with Father Oglesby. He and Sue were involved in just about everything: Adult education, the Youth programs, the Liturgy, and music. Ken was not a difficult person to get to know. He was an easy person to like.

I thought I knew him pretty well, but then a marriage in the family revealed a side I'd never known. I discovered at that wedding rehearsal that Ken was into control. But he was on my turf, and I was also into control. It seemed, as I recall, that Ken had ideas about almost everything, and most of them differed from what I had in mind. And, of course, my ideas were not only correct, but the best.

We exchanged a word or two, and I told him time and again, *"Ken, go sit down."* But there was that thing between us that kept us from really being angry with each other, or staying upset. I guess you'd call it friendship. I'm sure I would. It took a while for me to learn the wisdom of the Church in appointing the priest as the *Official witness of the Church* at a wedding, and not the official arranger. Every now and then I find that I'm still learning it. But Ken learned his lesson about control — he died in the morning, just as the day was getting started, and things needed to be planned.

I remember some years ago, we put one over on him. Sue and I did it, but there were many others involved. It was his 50th birthday, and Sue had planned a surprise party. It was to be celebrated in the Narthex of Nativity Church. I had only recently moved into the new rectory. Never doubt that Ken played a part in the construction of both the rectory and the church building of Nativity. So Sue and I planned a ruse that was bound to work. At the appointed time, when Sue and Ken were enjoying a quiet birthday observance at home, I called and asked if Ken would come to the property because I kept smelling smoke in the church building. I told him that I'd wait for him in the rectory since I didn't want to discover a fire in the church building without some help.

Ken arrived more quickly than I expected, so much did he love Nativity. I felt I had to delay him to give Sue time to join our fellow conspirators in the Narthex. So I took time to explain to him exactly where and when I'd smelled the smoke. I really enjoyed this, because Ken was not in charge and had no way of being in charge. How odd of Ken to have died at nine in the morning, just as the day was getting started, when so many things needed to be planned.

When it came time to celebrate my 25th anniversary of ordination, I could think of no better person to take charge than Ken and Sue. I remember that first meeting. There would never be another celebration like the one Ken had in mind. But then my illness took control. I had to leave and there was no celebration. We met again to plan it for the next year, but my change of assignments took it out of Ken's hands.

From my new assignment at St. Joseph I kept in touch with Ken and Sue. With other friends we'd meet now and then for lunch at Red Lobster. His cancer stole his appetite and robust appearance, but he was still in charge. He wore a jaunty beret with a symbol of the Holy Spirit on it. He never lost his smile, and his concern for others. How sad, I thought, that he should die at nine in the morning, just as the day was getting started with so many a thing to plan.

I visited several times during those last days of his life. We talked of death and dying, of fear and forgiveness. He, and Sue, and I prayed the rosary together. I asked him, *"What mysteries would you like?"* With a tired smile he looked at me and said, *"Let's pray the Joyful mysteries, Father."* And so we did. The next time it was the Glorious mysteries. We never did pray the Sorrowful ones.

I told him on one of those visits, *"Ken, I'm gonna give a talk on faith at the next Men's Cursillo, what should I tell them?"* He thought a bit and said, almost in a whisper, *"Tell them not to try so hard to get it."* I thought it was a strange answer, especially coming from Ken. I asked him, *"Do you mean it's a gift from God, not something we earn?"* He shook his head affirmatively, *"Yeah, that's it."* This was Ken, who always worked so hard to have things just right and always thought he had to.

Come to think of it, it's not so strange that Ken died at nine in the morning. He'd had his family around him the night before. That would have been the perfect time — the kind of thing that Ken would have arranged. But Ken was no longer in charge, and he'd known that for some time. Somewhere along the road he'd made a decision to do it HIS way, not Ken's way. He didn't quit, but he did surrender. To quit says, *"I can't do this."* To surrender says, *"I can't do this alone."* Ken surrendered to his God.

44 — A LESSON IN LETTING GO

Well Lent has started, and that's a fact, but is it a fact that I've started on Lent?

On Ash Wednesday when I talked to my people, I suggested a two-fold effort for Lent. Neither of the two had to do with *"giving up"* anything. The two suggestions were: 1) Work on relationships; and 2) Read a book or two.

A week or so ago, I stopped by to see a good friend of mine, Father Ed Byrnes. During the course of our conversation he recommended a book that had just hit the market, *The Gift of Peace* by Cardinal Bernardin, the late Archbishop of Chicago. Usually I'm not inclined to read books by Cardinals. I figure they're way above my head, or too filled with *"churchy"* language, but Father Byrnes made it sound down to earth, and interesting.

When I stopped by St. Paul Book and Media I had forgotten the name of the book but I found it with ease since it was prominently displayed. It's only 153 pages. It concerns itself with the last three years of the Cardinal's life. He wrote this little volume with full knowledge that he was dying of pancreatic cancer. It's divided into four parts, but it's all about, "letting go." I'm a slow reader, but I could have easily read the book in a day. Francis Bacon, a philosopher and man of letters in the late 1500's wrote, *"Some books are to be tasted, others to be swallowed, and some few to be chewed and digested."* This book falls into the last category.

As I write this, I've finished the first part of the book, but I'll not start the second part until next week. I want to chew on this first part, and digest for a while. It deals with the episode of the false accusation of sexual abuse against the Cardinal. It deals with one of the things that I find difficult to do — to let go of something that's worrying me, to put it fully in the hands of the Lord.

The Cardinal doesn't tell me how to do it. He does tell me how he did it. He tells me of the difficulties he endured while trying to let go. He shares his experience without judging mine. I can almost hear him repeating a phrase I've heard very often: *"If you want what I've got, do what I did."* But he also seems to say, *" Do what I did, but do it your way."*

So far the book is full of tenderness, but not so as to turn off a man looking for a challenge. It is without compromise when it comes to the need to *let go*, to turn things over to God, never-the-less, it freely recognizes the individual ways and means of *letting go*.

I'm going to read this book for Lent. This reminds me of what a teacher of mine used to say whenever I seemed to challenged him by saying, *"But I read a book that said....."* That teacher would smile at me and say, *"That's nice, now go read another one."* So I think I'll read a few books for Lent.

About relationships and Lent. I have some close friends, some just plain friends, and some acquaintances. I also have some relationships that I've ignored, or are in a shaky condition. I think Lent will be a good time for me to look at all my relationships and see how I can make them better. It's time that I looked to see where Christ is in these relationships.

When I look at the Scriptures and see the many relationships into which Jesus entered, I see two things that are common to all of them. First: He enjoyed each person for whoever they were. Second: He was always aware that His mission was to make each person He met aware of the Father's love. To make each person he met aware that reconciliation with the Father was possible, available, and desirable.

What I'd like to do this Lent is look at my relationships with others in that same light. This can not be a matter of saccharin and sugar. To know that, I've only to look at the encounter between Jesus and the very macho man who had taken refuge among the tombs. (Mk 5:1-20). Looking at the meeting of Jesus with the woman taken in adultery, I know that none of my relationships can ever be a "holier than thou" thing. Jesus related to so many different people: Zacchaeus, the rich tax collector; Bartimaeus, the blind beggar: Mary, His mother; Dismas the thief with whom He was crucified; His apostles; Martha, Mary and Lazarus.

It seems to me that Jesus accepted each person He met just as they were. He didn't seek to change them, yet to each He offered an opportunity for change that was, and is, growth.

Well, now it's out. I'm not giving up anything for Lent. I'm gonna read a few books, and work on relationships. Something tells me this is gonna involve *letting go* of attitudes and things. There just seems to be no way out of it — I'm gonna end by giving up more than I'm ready for now.

45 — FIGHTING WITH THE LIFE GUARD

I had an unusual conversation with a friend of mine the other day, and I thought I'd share it with you. I'll call this friend John, but that's not his real name. I'd better tell you from the outset that I have his permission to share this.

John told me of a life guard who was sued by a man he'd rescued from drowning. It seems the victim put up a stiff fight when the life guard tried to help him. His panic and fear was so great that the life guard feared both he and the victim would drown, so he knocked him out. In the process, he accidentally broke the man's jaw. So the victim sued. The case was pending, and John didn't know how it turned out.

It was at this point that the conversation took such an unusual turn. John told me, "Ya know, I can sympathize with that drowning man. There are times when I've been drowning in a sea of temptations, and I didn't recognize the lifeguard the Lord sent me. I'd get panicked and frightened, and put up a pretty good fight. Sometimes, to get my attention, the lifeguard the Lord sent demanded I let go of a social or business relationship. An the whole thing is like the swimmer who got his jaw broken, and sometimes I feel like suing."It's like the life guard who had to break the swimmer's jaw to save him. And, ya know what, I often feel like suing."

John told me that the drowning victim would probably swear that he wasn't that bad off, and there was no need for the lifeguard to have gotten so violent with him — and he could relate to that.

"That's what I like about Lent," he continued, "It gives me a chance to get my life in some kind of order before I have to face the Lord, my real Lifeguard. It's like getting things in order at work before OSHA shows up, or like picking up around the house before the maid comes in. Ya know what I mean, Father?"

I gotta admit that I did, indeed, know what John was talking about. Before I face the Lord with this or that particular problem in my life, I want to know that I can live life as it'll be with the Lord's solution. Before I holler, *"Help!!"*, before I, *"Go to confession,"* I want the Lord to know that I got things under control. In other words, I want the Lord to save me when I'm in shallow water, not when I'm in over my head. For some crazy reason, this seems to make me feel better, or at least look better.

John asked, *"What's the point of going to confession if ya know you're going right back to the same thing?"* I told John that Jesus had addressed that very question, but from the other side of the coin. Remember when the Pharisees got all upset with Jesus because of who he went to dinner with? *"He eats with sinners!"* Jesus simply replied, *"Those who are well do not need a doctor, but sick people do."* (Mt. 9:12)

In my experience as a human being, I've discovered that many people, myself included, generalize, or minimize whenever we can. The theory seems to be: if I can just get the information on how to handle this little thing, I'll be able to apply it to the big thing that's really bothering me, and no one will think I'm as bad off as I am. That's something like asking for information to treat a sprained ankle, when you've really got a broken leg.

This reminds me of the story of the alcoholic whose wife was trying to get him into treatment. She told him that he had missed the driveway three times last week, and parked the car in the middle of the yard, and once on the porch. The lawn is littered with empty bottles and beer cans, and several people had called the police to complain about his loud singing at three in the morning. She concluded by saying, *"Don't you think you should get some professional help to deal with this problem?"* He looked at her with all seriousness and said, *"You might be right, hon, but what would the neighbors think if I went into treatment for alcoholism?"*

Father Rohr told me something a long time ago that has stuck with me. He said that he had finally admitted and come to grips with a problem he'd kept hidden for some years. One of his first reflections after admitting the problem was, *"Lord You've known about this problem all along, and You still loved me."*

I think John's right. Lent's a time to get my life in order. But I've got to remember Jesus said, "Come to me, all who are weary and heavily burdened." He didn't say, "Come to me all who have your life in order and under control." Besides, God already knows all about my problems. He's just waiting for me claim them as mine, so He can say, *"See, I still love ya."*

46 — WHAT'S SO REAL ABOUT MARY?

March 25th is the feast of the Annunciation. It's one of many momentous events in the history of our salvation. This year it fell during Holy Week so the Church has held off the celebration until after Easter. The feast is a very important one, so the Church doesn't just skip over it. In secular history the landing on the moon was a momentous event. On July 20, 1969 all the tools of the media recorded the event which was described as, *"One small step for (a) man and one giant leap for mankind."*

No one knows exactly how, or when the Annunciation took place. There were no TV, radio, or newspaper reporters around to capture the event. It never occurred to me to wonder why we celebrate the event on March 25th. When I was in the seminary one of my professors let the cat out of the bag, and I got a chuckle out of it. The Annunciation recalls the conception of Jesus within the womb of Mary, so, after the Church decided on a date to celebrate the Nativity, it simply counted nine months back to March 25th as the date of the Annunciation.

The *what* and *how* of the Annunciation are important. The *when* is not. The *what* is the conception of Jesus within the womb of Mary. The *how* is by the power of the Holy Spirit. I kinda think that there's also a *what else* and a *how else* to be considered. The *what* and the *how* tell me a great deal about God, and His will to save. The *what else* and the *how else* speak volumes about Mary — and her very humanness.

I can picture Mary as not noticeably different from many of her peers. She has this experience with an angel of the Lord, who tells her wondrous and exciting things that can happen, if she agrees to what God wants to do with, and for, her. Of course she agrees, and now comes the *what else.*

What is she going to do with this good news? The angel didn't say anything about keeping it a secret. My first impression is that Mary wanted to rush out and tell the world. Well, at least everyone she knew. Maybe she did tell a few people. If the experiences of the three children at Fatima and Bernadette at Lourdes tell me anything, I can almost see the unbelieving responses she got. Think about it. I mean, what would you do if your unmarried daughter, granddaughter, or niece came to you with the good news that she was going to have a baby, and not only that, but Holy Spirit of God was the Father, not her fiancee?

I've thought about it, and although I wouldn't say, *"Show me the money!"*, I'd be tempted to say, *"Show me the proof!!"* All of this has convinced me that Mary was not the saccharine ceramic that she is often pictured as. She was one tough gal.

I've often wondered if, after the experience with the angel of the Lord was over, Mary didn't begin to have second thoughts. Oh, not that she was about to change her mind. Perhaps she said to herself, *"Did this really happen? Was I just dreaming? Who's going to believe me? Oh, my God, what am I going to tell Joseph?"*

The scriptures have been so holy for so long for me that I tend to forget they deal with real people facing real situations. The people in the scripture, the saints of our traditions are good and holy people. Their holiness, however, is not their own — it's a gift of God that they accepted. And I suppose they accepted it as human beings, with a bit of fear and trepidation.

Mary is a person I can relate to, if I just let her be human. I can picture her having all kinds of questions after the angel Gabriel left. I can see her recalling that the angel told her that her cousin, Elizabeth, was also going to have a baby. "At her age?" "Besides that, she's sterile."

A man named Miguel de Anemone claimed in his *The Agony of Christianity*, "*Faith which does not doubt is dead faith..*" And Tennyson noted, "*There lives more faith in honest doubt, believe me, than in half the creeds.*" But before these two spoke, St. Paul, speaking of Abraham, our father in faith, said "*He believed, hoping against hope that he would become 'the father of many nations' according to what had been told him.*" (Romans 4:18) That's the way I understand Mary rushing off to see Elizabeth. She is going to help her cousin, of course, but she's also hoping against hope that what the angel told her is true. I can hear her saying to herself, "*I don't know what I'll tell Joseph, but I'll deal with that when I get back.*"

I've heard the Good News. At times it seems too good to be true. I've done nothing to deserve it, yet the Father sent his Son for me. Mary is a person I can relate to: Hoping against hope; believing in spite of anxieties; letting the future take care of itself, and dealing with the present reality. We delayed the celebration of the Annunciation, but it's worth celebrating.

47 — HOLD, PLEASE

Do you remember when you were a kid? Do you remember what you'd do when you heard your mom calling you? If you're anything like me, you'd linger as long as you dared, and then head for home. But then what?

In the June edition of the *Catholic Digest,* in a section called *"Words for Quiet Moments,"* Esther de Waal is quoted, "**Listen** *is the opening word of the Rule of St. Benedict.... If I am to be true to my calling, my vocation, I must go on listening for this voice. There is such a danger that I talk about God, and enjoy talking about God, and do not stop and in the silence of my heart listen to God speaking."*

I've written about vocations before, and tried to make it clear that I know there are many different kinds of vocations. I am convinced that God calls people to the diocesan priesthood, and to religious life. I'm also convinced that God calls people to marriage, and to a Christian celibacy that is distinct from priesthood, or religious life. Further, I'm convinced that He calls to people who are employers or employees in a multitude of differing pursuits.

The question I want to look at today, is not what God calls a person to, but what a person is likely doing in order to hear the call, and what they keep on doing after they have heard the call.

I think that God calls every one, and each one of us, and I think the call is continuous. A person is foolish who willingly stops learning after graduation. What a person learns in grade school, high school, college, business or professional school is simply the foundation — the tools to use to keep on learning.

Unfortunately, there are people who answer God's call by receiving the sacraments of initiation (Baptism, Holy Communion, and Confirmation) and think they've done it all. There are even some who answer God's call by receiving the sacraments of Matrimony or Holy Orders and consider the day of marriage or ordination as having accomplished it all. Any further calls from God, like — *"Hello Bill, this is God,"* are too often answered with, *"Hi God this is Bill, hold please."*

If you've ever called anyone and heard, *"Hello, this is so-n-so, hold please,"* you know how irritating that can be. Imagine putting God on hold.

I think St. Benedict was on to something by using **LISTEN** as the opening word of the Rule of St. Benedict.

Every profession I've heard of, from auto mechanic to brain surgeon, has mandatory updates, or refresher courses. There are management techniques for those in management. How to survive marriage seminars are there for those who want to work at making their marriage a success. The person who does not continue to study, to listen after graduation, marriage, or ordination, makes couch potatoes look active.

I'm writing this on a Saturday morning, and I just remembered that yesterday was the deadline for signing up for the Priest Study Days in June, and I forgot to sign up. So I've made a call to the priest in charge, and left a message. The message was that I forgot, and if there's still an opening, put me in it. If the Study Days were the only way of Listening, I'd really look bad. Thank God they're not, cause I don't need any help when it comes to looking bad — at least now and then.

Some people ask me why I put myself down like I just did. My answer is simply this: "If I do it first, it's easier to take, and I eliminate the opportunity, or desire, for anyone else to do it."

At the top of this column I asked if you remembered what your response was when your mom called you to come home. I then asked if you remembered what you did after you got home. What I did was find out what my mom wanted. She didn't simply call me to come home — she wanted me to do something.

I'm convinced that God has called me and you. He has called us to be His son or daughter. After that He calls us in many and varied ways. He calls us to be employers or employees, professionals or artists, even priests. As Fr. Knight pointed out recently, no matter what our profession, job, or whatever — we are first called to be His children. Especially children who continually listen for the voice of the Father in whatever we do.

48 — FORGIVE? HOW?

He looked like a little boy, but he wasn't. His face was streaked with tears and his eyes were red from lack of sleep, and from crying. It was at the funeral Mass that I saw him and gave him Communion. He looked like a little boy, but he wasn't. He was a man, and what a man he turned out to be!!

Greg Kuehl is his name, and when I saw him he had just recently lost his wife, his six month old daughter, and his unborn son. I had seen him on Friday night, the night it happened, the night of the accident. His little daughter Zadie was still alive then, but struggling for life at Le Bonheur Hospital. Stephanie, his wife, had died at the scene of the accident, and when she died, her unborn child, whom Greg named, Thomas Sterling Kuehl, also died.

Let me tell you about Greg and Stephanie, and in the telling you'll come to know what wonderful parents they've had.

Stephanie was just 24 when she died. She was the daughter of Dave and Margaret Brown. Sure, she was the daughter of the Memphis "TV Weather Man," but that was secondary to her. What was first, was what Dave and Margaret taught her, the values they shared with her. They taught her to love, to care about, and to give a smile to those who were hurting, or those who just needed one. They taught her to be willing to notice, to listen, to be one with the people around her. Stephanie became what she was taught.

She met a man named Greg with whom she had much in common, and she married him, and that was the happiest day of her life, until she had her first child, a daughter they named Zadie, and then, that was the happiest day of her life.

But her happy life — their happy lives — came to an abrupt end on Friday night, May 30th when Stephanie and Thomas were killed. And then Zadie died the next day at Le Bonheur. The driver who hit their car is now charged with vehicular homicide, drunken driving, driving on a revoked license, and reckless driving.

There is much material here for anger, for rage, for hate. Perhaps some would like to choke the life out of the one responsible for this disaster. There are those who fume inside, wanting to do something, but not knowing what to do, and so they cry.

Greg cried, but he also prayed. He knew God was with him so he listened for what God had in mind. Then he knew what he had to do, and he did it. In the doing of it, he showed what his parents had somehow taught him, and what he had in common with his wife, Stephanie.

Stephanie was always giving things away, and when Zadie died, Greg agreed to give her vital organs away. And now, five people in five different states have a better chance at life.

Early Monday morning Greg Kuehl made up his mind about what else he had to do, and he did it. He realized that love must overcome hate. He was convinced that, *"If I'm gonna get through this, I must forgive this guy."* He remembered what Jesus said as he hung dying on the cross, "Father forgive them for they know not what they do." Greg knew what he had to do, and he did it.

Being a long-time friend of the Kuehl family, and having officiated at Greg's and Stephanie's wedding, I was honored to speak at the cemetery. There was only one casket for Stephanie, Zadie, and Thomas — their unborn child. Before it was lowered into the ground, I shared Greg's thoughts, which Father Fisher had shared with me. Among the hundred or so people who were there, some seemed stunned.

"Forgive? How?"

I explained that forgiveness does not mean to relieve one of the responsibility for one's actions. No!! Not at all. Forgiveness means that I abandon the desire to hold a grudge. It means that I will not sully my soul and heart with thoughts of revenge. To forgive means that I set myself free from an unholy alliance with evil. Forgiveness does not mean that Greg dishonors the memory of his wife and children. No!! It means that he immerses that memory in the cleansing power of the love and mercy of God.

Often today when young people get into trouble of some sort, I hear people ask, "Why didn't their parents do something?" I'm never sure that's a valid question. But this much I do know: The Browns and the Kuehls did something with their children and it is glorious to behold!!

49 — A LESSON IN LIVING AND DYING

I've written to you about Jennie Ames, and how she died. Recently I wrote to you about Greg, and Stephanie Kuehl. I'm a little hesitant to write again about death, but this experience was such a rewarding one that I am going to do it anyway.

I first encountered Jim Handwerker when Fathers Al and Tom Kirk and I were counselors at Camp Marymount many years ago. Jim and Jerry Handwerker gave life and lessons to ten children. I met two of them at Camp. The parents let me know that their children were accustomed to obedience and discipline.

Many years later, after their children had grown up, and Jim had retired, I became reacquainted with Jim and Jerry. It is this acquaintance that I want to tell you about for it shows the remarkable character of Jim Handwerker.

When I came to St. Joseph parish in July of 1990, there were many who thought that St. Joseph was on the verge of closing. Some thought that it had already closed. Even at Jim's funeral, there were some who were surprised that St. Joseph was still open.

More than a few years back, Whitehaven, where St. Joseph is located, was a rapidly growing community. But something happened, something I'll not go into. The economic and racial character of the community changed. For various reasons, many people moved out of the area, but not Jim and his family. Jim stayed because this was his home, his parish, and it was the right thing to do.

Jim was a valid hero of World War II. He was Captain of the B-29 "City of Memphis," and recipient of the Silver Star. Perhaps you read about it in the paper recently. He was not a spur of the moment hero. He was simply a man who saw his duty and did it, because it was the right thing to do.

While at St. Joseph, Jim discovered a member of the parish with whom he had much in common, DeLester Williams. They both were pilots during the war, Jim a Captain, DeLester a Major. They both had a love for church, parish, community, and country. The difference between the two was that DeLester was Black and Jim was White. Never-the-less, a quality friendship flourished between them. This was not because Jim felt sorry, or guilty about the way the black pilots were treated during the war. I don't know if Jim ever felt sorry for anyone, but when right, or values were abused, Jim was more than just saddened. "Everybody's doing it." "We've always done it this way." These concepts were not part of Jim's philosophy when it came to right and wrong — to values. I guess that's why Jim and DeLester's friendship flourished — they had much in common. The night before Jim died, DeLester dropped by and they sang the old Air Corp songs together.

Jim knew he was dying. He had known for some time. He died of cancer. Many months ago he had part of his ear cut off in an effort to beat the cancer. The effort left him with half an ear on one side of his head. Some might think it unsightly, but not Jim. He had a beautiful stock of sliver white hair with which he could have covered it, but he didn't. For Jim there were things more important than outward appearances.

When the cancer was finally diagnosed as terminal, he matter-of-factly told the Finance Council of our parish about it. He told us that he didn't want any special fanfare, or treatment, he just thought he should tell us. He remained a member of the Council until the day he died.

During the last months of his life on earth, I visited him often. I had Mass, with his family gathered around, in his home twice. I asked him one morning when I brought Holy Communion, *"Jim, are you worried about anything? Are you afraid?"*

Jim looked up at me from his chair, smiled a bit, and said, *"No, Father, I'm not worried about anything. I'm not afraid of dying."* But then he thought a while and added, *"But that doesn't make me a brave, or courageous man. I'm just a man who trusts the Lord."*

That wasn't a spur of the moment trust. It was a process of a lifetime's way of living. Jim taught his children a lot about how to live. He taught them more about how to die.

You may be interested to know that the Mayors of Memphis and Shelby County prepared and delivered a proclamation that made June 4th, 1997 *"Jim Handwerker Day"*. Jim used that day to go home. He was a hero of World War II, and we buried him on June 6th — D-Day.

50 — DAT'S MY DADDY!!

Abba, please help me to share with others what You have shared with me.

Some people have asked me if it's difficult to write a column each week. Sometimes it's easy and sometimes it's difficult, very difficult. Some months ago, when it was especially difficult I started the column with the opening line you see above. When I finished the column, I deleted it. Since that time I've begun every column that way. I thought I'd leave that line in today, because it's part of what Abba has shared with me.

"Abba" is a Hebrew word, and as far as I know, it means something like what we express when we use the word "Daddy." It's the way a child speaks to his or her male parent. "Abba" is used three times in the New Testament: Mark 14:36; Romans 8:15; and Galatians 4:6.

In the agony in the Garden of Gethsemane the night before He died, Mark tells me that Jesus, knowing what was coming His way, prayed, *"Abba, Father, all things are possible to you. Take this cup away from me, but not what I will but what You will."*

In Paul's letter to the Romans he writes of the great honor we've been given. *"For you did not receive a spirit of slavery to fall back into fear, but you received a spirit of adoption, through which we cry, Abba, Father."* When I read that, I think of the words from the song in the musical **Oliver**, "Consider yourself part of the family, consider yourself at home." That's what Abba means to me.

In his letter to the Galatians, Paul says, *"As proof that you are children, God sent the spirit of His Son into our hearts, crying out, 'Abba', Father!"* For a long time I thought that the word "Father" was added as an explanation of the word Abba. And I guess it was. But I kinda think that whoever added it was a little afraid of the informality of the word, "Abba." Sure, Abba means Father in the same way that daddy means father. But just as daddy means a whole lot more than just father, so also Abba means a whole lot more than just father.

I've known about "Abba" for quite a long time now, but only in the last few years has it become an important. and vital, element in my spiritual growth. I was reading one of Herman Wouk's novels about the establishment of the modern state of Israel. It was either, *The Hope*, or *The Glory*. Some of the children, even young adults, in the stories just naturally called their male parent, "Abba." That experience helped me to see the word, "Abba," in scripture as real and living.

It may seem strange to some people for a 65 year old man to be calling out for his daddy, his Abba, but it makes perfect sense to me. I know that God is with me at all times. God's everywhere. But when Abba is with me, that's something else. I might be intimidated by the fact that my Father is watching me, but not so with Abba. Sometimes the relationship is so truly felt that I want to cry out, "Look at me Daddy, look at me Abba!"

With all of the really serious problems this world has, it's easy to get the very human idea that God has a whole lot of other — or more important stuff — to be concerned about than my little, or even my big problems. But whether my problems are big, or little, my Abba is never too busy.

In a way it's astounding to realize that although I admire, respect, and like our Bishop, I'd never feel comfortable referring to him in any way except Bishop Steib, or perhaps Bishop Terry, but I'm quite at ease calling God, Abba.

Sometimes when we talk about religion, or things spiritual, it's done with about as much feeling as when we're describing pieces of flatware for the dining room table. It's technical and correct. A couple of months ago I was talking with a little friend of mine. His name is Ryan Patrick, and he's just over two years of age. I pointed to a picture of a young man who's also a friend, and ask, *"Who's that, Ryan."* Ryan looked at the picture, and with a smile as big as his face said, *"Dat's my daddy!!"*

God is certainly Father to me, and that means a whole lot. He's also Abba to me. As Ryan said, *"Dat's my daddy!!"* and that means a whole lot more.

51 — DEATH WITH DIGNITY, OR DIGNITY WITH DEATH

Death with Dignity. Just what does that mean? Some say Dr. Kevorkian provides Death with Dignity. My purpose is not to argue with them, nor is it to tear down their point of view. I seek to find another way of looking at Death and Dignity. I seek to find a person who strives to provide, not Death with Dignity, but Dignity with Death. I don't think I'm just playing with words, I'm putting the emphasis on Dignity, not Death. I think I've found such a person.

Some say that all Dr. K does is relieve a person's pain and suffering and bring a conclusion to a meaningless life. That attitude cheapens life, it does not enhance it. From what I understand this is what happens:

A person who has a terminal illness, and is sick and tired of suffering and pain, and is leading a meaningless life seeks out Doctor K. He counsels with the person, and if he agrees that life is meaningless, he puts the person up in an inexpensive motel, or the back of a van. The doctor has built a contraption of cans, and chemicals, and tubes. When used properly, the fumes put the person into a death sleep. The doctor simply instructs the person in its use, and then watches to make sure they do it right. And this is Death with Dignity?

The person I've found doesn't wait to be called. This person goes out into the streets and the alleys looking for people who are sick and tired of pain and suffering, and leading a meaningless life. This person then provides a clean bed and the suffering person is bathed, and fed, and nourished, and more than that, much more than that, the person is caressed and loved — and the spiritual needs of that person are met. Not just for the day, but for life. A meaningless life is given meaning. Now this, this is Dignity with Death.

With Doctor K the attitude seems to be: Hey, there's no need for you to suffer all this much. Your life's about over anyway. You're never gonna get any better. Where's the meaning to your life? You might as well get it over with. It's better than being a burden to others.

With the person I've found the attitude is: Hey, there's no need for you to suffer alone. The end may be near, but we're in this together. Your life is a precious gift of God, and therefore it has great meaning. You're no burden to me. You are, in Christ, brother and sister, mother and father to me. Together we are family. You're a call from God, who loves us both.

A person who is terminally ill and suffering, if left alone will soon, and very soon, come to think that life and pain have no meaning or value. And the best thing is to be done with it.

If that person is left alone with Doctor K., that type of thinking will be confirmed, and death by way of his contraption will be seen as a blessing, as Death with Dignity.

If someone terminally ill is left alone with the person I've found, he or she will soon, and very soon, discover that he or she is not alone. This dying person will know that life has meaning and value, despite pain and suffering — simply because they'll know they are loved. And that is Dignity with Death.

I guess, by now, you've figured out I'm talking about Mother Teresa.

What's to be done about Doctor K.? The courts can't seem to get a conviction. Perhaps a new law, or two, will do the job. Like they say when luck makes a 7-10 split in bowling — *"It looks good on paper!"* I don't think the problem will be solved by restraining, or imprisoning Dr. K. I think the only real solution is to replace his way of thinking.

For those of us who strive not only to teach as Jesus did, but to think as Jesus did, Mother Teresa and others have given us an example. It's not enough to admire her, because that, as they say in bowling, only *"Looks good on paper."*

We can not all do the things that Mother Teresa and her sisters do. And I'm sure that we do not all do the things that Dr. K. does. I'm also convinced that we don't all have the talents or the time to argue the merits of one side or the other. Of this much I am certain: We all can, and do, have an attitude.

When I consider Dr. K, and his Death with Dignity, and Mother Teresa, and her Dignity with Death, I know where I want to form my attitude. I hope you do.

52 — DON'T BOTHER ME!!

Perhaps you've heard this passage from John's Gospel, *"Peace I leave with you; my peace I give to you. Not as the world gives do I give it to you."* (Jn 14:27)

For many years I'd preached to the people about what I understood as the difference between the Peace of the Lord, and the Peace of the World. For me what the world had to offer was an absence of war, or fighting, or arguments.

The Lord had much more to offer. It wasn't characterized by the absence of anything. I had little real understanding of exactly what the positive aspects of that Peace were other than the Peace of a good conscience and the conviction of God's love for me.

Then, a few years ago someone came out with a greeting he used at the exchange of the Sign of Peace during Mass. His greeting was, *"May the Peace of Christ profoundly disturb you."* What he was getting at was that the Peace of Christ was something more than a warm, fuzzy, feel good thing.

To be profoundly disturbed by the Peace of Christ, meant that I would have to be shaken out of whatever complacency I, with or without purpose, had wandered into.

The other day I started reading an article in the **Catholic Dossier** for September-October 1997. The article was titled, "Mother Teresa Addresses America." She gave this address at the 1994 National Prayer Breakfast attended by President and Mrs. Clinton.

What she had to say about that passage from John's Gospel opened my eyes a bit wider. "He came not to give the peace of the world, which is only that, we don't bother each other. He came to give the peace of heart, which comes from loving — from doing good to others."

I laughed a bit at the absurdity, and yet firm grip, on the reality of what the peace of the world meant to her: *don't bother anybody!!!* WOW!!! I was sobered by the stark simplicity of her understanding of the Peace of Christ: *"The Peace of heart which comes from loving — from doing good to others."*

A few years ago, I wrote of a scene in which Jesus addressed the leaders of the world who were seeking peace. All He said to them was, "Little children love one another." The leaders of the world mumbled to themselves, "He just doesn't understand." But all they said to Him was, "Have your people fax our people. Keep in touch." In 1994, Mother Teresa stood before the President of the United States, some say the most powerful man in the world, and told him what was disturbing the peace and how to find peace.

She spoke of how much time busy parents were spending maintaining a standard of living and how little time they were spending loving their children. *"We are talking of love of the child which is where love and peace must begin. These are the things that break the peace." ".... the greatest destroyer of peace today is abortion, because it is war against the child."* She said that we must be willing to convince the mother that she is loved, that there are people who care, that there is hope. We must be willing to help the mother **and father** of the child to give until it hurts his and her plans, or his and her free time, and help them to accept and carry out their responsibilities.

Mother Teresa spoke of the violence in our country and the concern many people have in this regard, but she said there was little concern for the millions who are being killed by the deliberate decision of their own mothers (and often the deliberate lack of concern by their fathers). She said that abortion is the greatest destroyer of peace today, because it brings people to a blindness and callousness about so many other forms of violence.

Some may think it's easy for Mother Teresa to speak of giving up this and giving up that since she has never been married and has little understanding of the stress and demands of married life. Well, a professor in the United States asked her, "Are you married?" Mother replied, "Yes, and I find it sometimes very difficult to smile at my spouse, Jesus, because He can be very demanding — sometimes."

As anyone knows who knows even a little about Mother Teresa, the demands of her spouse, Jesus, are total. She was to love Him in everyone she met. The Peace of Christ is, "Love one another."

The peace of the world is, *"Don't bother me!!"*

Afterword

WHY SHOULD GOD REMEMBER ME?

The thoughts for the following meditation came to me in the summer of 1982 when, it seemed, an unusual number of prominent people died. Prominent friends of theirs would be called together by one of the many TV news' shows to recall things about the deceased. The question of how one would like to be remembered was frequently asked. The same question is often asked of people who are retiring.

While considering this, it occurred to me that being remembered is not all that important, if one is not remembered by God. I asked myself, "Why should God remember me?"

That verse from Isaiah came to mind and gave me comfort, *"Can a mother forget her infant, be without tenderness for the child of her womb? Even should she forget, I will never forget you."* (Isaiah 49:15) That tells me that God will remember me — but not **why**.

I put my thoughts on paper, and now I share them with you in a meditation I have entitled:

WHY SHOULD GOD REMEMBER ME?

"How would you like to be remembered?" The question often asked of people who are retiring, or who have the fullness of years.

I've seen them ask it on the evening news. I've often wanted to answer that question. And I've wondered why no one ever answered it the way I would.

How would I like to be remembered? "Frankly my dear, I don't give a damn."

EXCEPT, except that *God* remember me.

And then I stare, and I ponder, and I wonder, "Why should *God* remember me?" I've not shook the pillars of society, nor even caused a ripple in the sea. So, why should God remember me?

My study of the scripture has been interrupted by naps and TV. My well-formed plan to delve deeper into theology has suffered from my lack of constancy. So why on earth should God remember me?

I have discovered that I have a talent for this or that, but often not the will to follow through. It seems that every time I get some good idea, some one else must make it do. Why, oh why, should God remember me?

I've never fed a multitude, or multiplied the fish and loaves. I've only fed a couple here and there, they never came in droves. "Is that enough?" I ask myself, and I know it's not, so why, why should God remember me?

I've never cured the sick, opened the ears of the deaf, or the eyes of the blind, Why should God remember me?

My prayer? I've prayed at Mass, and prayed at home. I've prayed at football games, and funerals, and every time I'm asked. I've prayed my heart, and when my heart was cold I prayed from memory, figuring that somehow God would understand. But it's all so routine, again I ask, "Why should God remember me?"

And now the answer comes, as it has come before. I know the answer well. I've heard it so very often. It's so simple, and yet so hard to believe. And now I'll tell the answer, the answer God gives me when I ask, "Why should God remember me?"

"Because I love you, Bill, and remember, I love you not for what you've done, but for who you are. You are My son, My own Son has made you so. See to it, that you remember that, and I will remember you."

.... and then, one day when I was old, and about to retire. There was a party, and all that stuff, and finally, finally the reporter asked, "Father, now that you are retiring, how would you like to be remembered after all these years?"

And I replied, "Frankly my dear, I don't give a damn."

The response I suggest is: SIRACH 44:1-15.

INDEX

AA (Alcoholics Anonymous) ... 70
Abba (daddy) ... 153-155
abortion ... 129-130, 161
acceptance ... 25-26, 28-29, 112-113
Adam & Eve ... 47
addiction ... 16-17, 52, 103, 130
adultery ... 81, 87, 137
alcohol ... 46, 103, 129-130, 139-140
Ames, Jennie ... 150
anger ... 39-41, 73, 132, 148-149
Annunciation ... 114-115, 141
anxiety ... 59, 143
arrogance ... 59, 69
attitudes ... 51-53, 137, 157-158
authority ... 106-107
awareness ... 112-113, 136
Bacon, Francis ... 135
beauty ... 21-23, 33-35
Bernardin, Cardinal ... 135
Bernstein, Leonard ... 112
betrayal ... 68
Bradley, Senator Bill ... 96-98
Brown, Dave & Margaret ... 147-149
burdens ... 64, 140, 157
Byrnes, Fr. Ed ... 135
Carley, Rev Burton ... 78
caution (prudence) ... 54
change ... 28-29, 101, 112, 137
charity ... 8, 75-76
cheating ... 46
children ... 24, 73-74, 78, 101, 108,
    126-127, 146, 149, 154, 160
Christmas ... 36, 39-41, 104, 114-116,
    121
Church of the Nativity ... 41
codependency ... 45
compassion ... 19, 71, 73
complacency ... 159
complicating the simple ... 127

confession ... 139
conscience ... 131, 159
control (see power)
coping ... 28, 55
covetousness ... 99
creation ... 21, 95
Daniel ... 87
David, King ... 46-47
death ... 4, 24-26, 39-41, 118, 120,
    122, 123-125, 126-128,
    132-134, 147-149, 150-152,
    156-158, 162
de Mello, Anthony ... 6, 23, 97, 112
de Waal, Esther ... 144
denial ... 15-17
devil ... 108-109
DeWitt, Ken ... 132-134
dignity ... 21, 156-158
disasters ... 57, 124-125, 148
discipline ... 11, 150-151
discouragement, disappointment ...44,
    51, 124
Divine (nature) Divinity ...59, 89, 116
doubt ... 143
drugs ... 46, 130
Easter ... 81, 85, 108, 141
embarrassment ... 70
failure ... 55, 57, 67, 70
faith ... 95, 110, 113, 143
Fatima ... 142
faults ... 102-104
fear ... 10-11, 28, 54-56, 73, 79-80, 83,
    110, 134, 138, 142, 152, 153
feelings ... 63, 112
forgetfulness ... 84-85, 123, 145-146
forgiveness ... 19, 71, 83, 134, 147-149
Frank, Anne ... 31, 68
freedom ... 102-104, 105, 130
friendship ... 105, 132, 136, 151-152

165

frustrations ... 59, 73
Gabriel ... 115, 142
Gandhi ... 31, 43, 44
gifts ... 43, 64, 106, 121-122, 134, 142
giving up ... 107, 135-137
grace ... 43, 66-67, 75, 77, 106, 111-113, 121-122
gratitude ... 76
grief ... 41
guilt ... 71, 76, 109-110, 131
gullibility ... 62
Handwerker, Jim & Jerry ... 150-152
happiness ... 27-29
hate ... 148
hell ... 30, 63-64
Holleran, Msgr. Warren ... 3
Holy Spirit ... 108-110, 115, 129, 133, 141-142
honesty ... 7-8, 62, 68
hope ... 143
hopelessness ... 52
human nature (humanness) ... 13, 97-98, 111-113, 116, 139, 141-143
humility ... 42-44, 119
Humphrey, Hubert ... 81
ignorance ... 69, 74
injustice ... 74
insecurity ... 70
intolerance ... 62
Isaiah ... 67, 83, 162
Jackson, Fr. Jay ... 30
Jeremiah ... 103
John ... 18, 20, 127, 159-160
John the Baptizer ... 114-116
Jolly, Billy ... 82-83
joy ... 50
Jung, Carl ... 105
justice ... 75-77, 126
Kennedy, Robert ... 73-74
Kevorkian, Dr. ... 156-158
King, Dr. Martin Luther ... 31, 42, 44, 68
Kirk, Fr. Al ... 127, 150

Kuehl, Greg, Stephanie, & Thomas ... 147-149, 150
Lent ... 48-50, 81, 135-137, 139-141
letting go ... 135-137
life ... 93
listening ... 144-146
Lombardi, Vince ... 45
Lourdes ... 142
love ... 22-23, 30, 37-38, 52-53, 65, 66, 76-77, 87-88, 97, 101, 119, 122, 126, 140, 148-149, 157-158, 159, 164
lying ... 46, 56, 87
Magy (& other family members) ... 39-41
Mark ... 153
Marx, Karl ... 53
Mary ... 41, 115-116, 137, 141-143
Mascari, Tony ... 82
McAuliffe, Christa ... 96, 98
meanness ... 69-70
meekness ... 42-44
Menninger, Karl ... 46, 85
Memphis ... 58
minimizing ... 139
money ... 58
Mother Teresa ... 35, 42, 34, 65, 115, 157-158, 159-161
Nativity scenes ... 39-41
necessities ... 105
obligations ... 36-38
Oglesby, Father ... 132
old age ... 94
openness ... 68, 92
ordinary things ... 102-104, 119
ordination ... 90, 133
pain ... 22, 41, 55, 67, 156-158
Paraclete ... 108-110
parents ... 72-74, 147-149
Parker, Dorothy ... 54
patience ... 60
Patrick, Ryan ... 155

Paul ... 10, 18-19, 43, 47, 53, 81-82, 85, 88, 99-101, 102, 106, 113, 118, 129-130, 143, 153
peace ... 19-20, 25-26, 56, 74, 126, 159-161
Peck, Scott ... 53
peer pressure ... 46
penance ... 48-50, 109
perfection ... 8
Peterson, David ... 119
politics ... 96-98
power & control (in relationships and experiences) ... 27-29, 31, 34, 44, 61, 106-107, 132-134, 139-140
prayer ... 11, 32, 56, 61, 134, 163-164
prejudice ... 14, 69, 78-80
priorities ... 19-20
prostitution ... 129-131
readiness ... 92
reality ... 34, 98, 104, 107, 109, 112-113, 125, 143, 160
reconciliation ... 137
relationships (with others & God) ... 13, 24, 65, 97, 111-113, 116, 121-122, 126, 135-137, 154
religion ... 6, 95, 144, 155
repentance ... 131
responsibility ... 123-124
revenge (and forgiveness) ... 149
Rice, Grantland ... 45, 47
Rhor, Father Richard ... 22, 64, 68, 75, 76, 80, 94, 105, 125, 140
sacred ... 100
saint (declaring one as) ... 100-101
Sanders, Red ... 45
secrets ... 10, 140
self-image ... 23, 70, 105-106
St. Francis of Assisi ... 35, 42, 44,
St. Theresa ... 65
selfishness ... 61, 73

serenity ... 25-26, 28-29, 31
sex ... 46, 73
sickness ... 120-122
simplicity ... 128
sin ... 16-17, 47, 67, 75, 83, 84-85, 97, 99, 102, 105, 110, 139
Slater, Philip ... 27, 29
spirituality (journey) ... 2, 6-8, 9-11, 29, 36, 53, 81, 86, 100-101, 102-104, 116, 128, 155, 157-158
stealing ... 46
Steib, Bishop Terry ... 155
strengths ... 62, 107
suffering ... 60, 68, 85, 88, 103, 156-158
Sullivan, Harry ... 90
surrender ... 71, 107, 134
Tabb, John Bannister ... 113
teaching ... 5, 91, 96-98
temper ... 103
temptations ... 44, 138-140
Teresa, Mother ... (see Mother Teresa)
Thomas, Lerleen ... 82
tragedies ... 31-32, 39-41, 57, 72-74, 126-127, 147-149
trust ... 50, 56, 73, 87-89, 152
truth ... 7, 35, 66, 100, 109-110
understanding ... 7, 103, 118, 121
values ... 151-152
vanity ... 91
violence ... 42-44, 74, 75, 160-161
weakness ... 67, 84-86, 105, 107
wealth ... 27-29
Wharton, Edith ... 66
Williams, DeLester ... 151-152
willingness ... 68, 92, 101, 112
wisdom ... 96, 122, 128
winning ... 45-46, 104
wonderful things prepared ...118-119
worrying ... 124-125, 136
worthiness ... 112

167